Tilli-
Thank you for sharing
all that you have here
in Hershey! We shall work
out just how your witness
model might best work here.
In hopes that this historical
venture into WWII will be
of interest. Through it, it is
a pleasure to introduce you
to my father.
Until next time, with
loving regards,
ZhL
Hershey, PA March 08

A Paratrooper's Panoramic View

Training with the 464th Parachute Field Artillery Battalion for Operation Varsity's 'Rhine Jump' with the 17th Airborne Division

By

Robert L. Wilson & Philip K. Wilson

authorHOUSE™

1663 LIBERTY DRIVE, SUITE 200
BLOOMINGTON, INDIANA 47403
(800) 839-8640
WWW.AUTHORHOUSE.COM

First published by AuthorHouse 11/29/05

ISBN: 1-4208-5429-1 (sc)

Printed in the United States of America
Bloomington, Indiana

This book is printed on acid-free paper.

Affectionately Dedicated to

The Memory of Every Paratrooper
In the 464th Parachute Field Artillery Battalion,
17th Airborne Division

Table of Contents

Introduction

The U.S. Paratrooper has added luster to the proud and honored traditions of the American fighting man.

General Matthew B. Ridgway, Paratrooper

To date, the WWII activities of only the 82nd and 101st Airborne Divisions have received considerable historical attention. Soon after WW II, James Gavin, who commanded the 82nd Airborne Division from their jump at Normandy through the end of the war, prepared a history of airborne operations that highlighted the activity of his division.[1] Recent accounts, including that of James Megellas have

---

[1] James M. Gavin's <u>Airborne Warfare</u> (Washington, DC: Infantry Journal Press, 1947), as well as his <u>On to Berlin: Battles of an Airborne Commander 1943-1946</u> (New York: Viking, 1978).

incorporated the idea of writing history "from below," that is, written not only from the commander's viewpoint but from a soldier's view. Work like Megellas' has provided considerable insight into the common soldier's experiences during WW II as part of the 82nd Airborne.[2]

More recently, attention has turned to the 101st Airborne due to Steven Ambrose's bestselling book and the accompanying Hollywood miniseries, Band of Brothers. Besides this work, an appreciation of life in the 101st during WW II may be gleaned from works by Richard Killblane, Jake McNeice, Donald R. Burgett, Robert Jones, Robert Bowen, Mark Bando, and David Kenyon Webster.[3]

Each of these divisions was important, as were the 11th, the 13th, and the 17th in gaining Allied victories in WW II. Perhaps future histories will acknowledge specific contributions that each of these divisions made in new writings on airborne action. For the most accurate representation, however, the airborne forces must always be considered as only part of the entire forces involved in outmaneuvering the Axis.

---

[2] James Megellas's All the Way to Berlin: A Paratrooper in World War II Europe (New York: Ballantine, 2003). See also Robert P. Anzuoni's The All American: An Illustrated History of the 82nd Airborne Division, 1917 to the Present (Atglen, PA: Schiffer Military History, 2001), Tim Saunders, Nijmegen: Market Garden – U.S. 82nd Airborne Division, 1944 (Barnsley, U.K.:Pen and Sword, 2001), Mark J. Nelson, With the Black Devils: A Soldier's WWII Account with the First Special Service Force and the 82nd Airborne (Atglen, PA: Schiffer Military History, 2003), Dominique François, 82nd Airborne in Normandy: A History in Period Photographs (Atglen, PA: Schiffer Military History, 2004), and Martin K.A. Morgan, Down To Earth: The 50th Parachute Infantry Regiment in Normandy, June 6-July 11, 1944 (Atglen, PA: Schiffer Military History, 2004).

[3] Richard Killblane and Jake McNeice, The Filthy Thirteen: From the Dustbowl to Hitler's Eagles Nest: The 101st Airborne's Most Legendary Squad of Combat Paratroopers (Havertown, PA: Casemate, 2003), and Donald R. Burgett's three works, Currahee: A Paratrooper's Account of the Normandy Invasion (New York: Bantam, 1999), Beyond the Rhine: A Screaming Eagle in Germany (New York: Presidio, 2001), and Road to Arnhem: A Screaming Eagle in Holland (New York: Dell, 2001). See also Robert Jones's 101st Airborne Division (Paducah, KY: Turner Publishing Co., 1997), Robert Bowen's Fighting with the Screaming Eagles: With the 101st Airborne Division from Normandy to Bastogne (Mechanicsburg, PA: Stackpole Greenhill Military Books, 2004), Mark A. Bando's Vanguard of the Crusade: The 101st Airborne Division in World War II (Bedford, PA: Aberjona, 2003), and David Kenyon Webster, Parachute Infantry: An American Paratrooper's Memoir of D-Day and the Fall of the Third Reich (New York: Delta, 2002).

When people find out that I jumped with an airborne unit, they frequently ask, "Was it the 82nd or the 101st?" When I answer, "Neither. I was with the 17th," they then ask, "Well, what did the 17th do?" Then I tell them.

This historical memoir recounts the story from one trooper's perspective that is placed within the context of paratrooper training and activity during WWII. Two people are responsible for the unfolding of this story: Robert, the trooper, who had the story to tell, and Philip, the historian, who faithfully crafted the narrative within a historical context. Still, throughout the book, the story is told in first person from the trooper's perspective.

Many others have also contributed to the production of this work over many years. Philip, when in high school, asked similar questions of his father (Robert) on many nights when gathered around the kitchen table after dinner. The seed of this book was undoubtedly planted at that time. Philip's sons, James and Douglas Wilson, regularly prodded "Papa" (Robert) to tell his tales again. James interviewed his grandfather, Robert, on several occasions, prompting several new recollections of WWII. James's interviews were incorporated into an essay, "A WWII Paratrooper's Story," which was among 297 entries submitted to the Hershey Museum's 2003-04 History Contest for Young Writers.[4] James's essay won the junior division (grades five and six) non-fiction category, gaining him, among other rewards, the "Willie Wonka Prize" — a private tour with his family through the Hershey Chocolate Factory in Hershey, Pennsylvania.

James's brother, Doug Wilson, had his grandfather, Robert, share some paratrooper adventures on Veterans' Day 2004 with his second grade class in Hershey Elementary School. The letters Robert received from students in response to his presentation ranged from extending thanks "for your service to protect our country" to it must have been "scary" but "cool" to be a paratrooper. Typically, they echoed second-grade teacher, Mrs. Katie Blum's remarks – "You made quite an impression on the children."

Fellow brothers of the 464th Parachute Field Artillery Battalion and others in the 17th Airborne Division have added much to the

---

[4] James C. Wilson, "A WWII Paratrooper's Story," essay submitted to the Hershey Museum's 2003-04 History Contest, Hershey, Pennsylvania.

story as they shared their own accounts with Robert at reunions held in recent years in Branson, Missouri, and Shreveport, Louisiana. Of these brothers, Charles Hewitt, Wade Hinson, Norvel "Luke" Lucas, and Ralph Williams have helpfully provided particular information. Wade Hinson offered his own written remembrances which have been included with due acknowledgement in this book.

464th Reunion, Shreveport, LA, 2003

Heartfelt thanks are also extended to the staff of the U.S. Army Military History Institute (USAMHI) and the U.S. Army War College in Carlisle, Pennsylvania. USAMHI's Dr. Richard J. Sommers initially ensured that we were furnished with the key sources, and Jim Baker and Gary Johnson were especially helpful in securing the needed material. It seemed appropriate to work on parachuting history in the new USAMHI quarters named in honor of Matthew B. Ridgway, the highest ranking paratrooper of WWII.

Dr. Michael J. Chorney, Professor of Microbiology and Immunology and Pediatrics at the Penn State College of Medicine in Hershey, Pennsylvania, enabled Robert and Philip to improve their telling of the story as he worked to get Robert included as a special guest at the 13th Annual World War II Weekend sponsored by the Mid Atlantic Air Museum and held June 4-6, 2004 in Reading, Pennsylvania. There, some of the 20,000 who attended this three-day weekend event heard Robert – dressed in his full trooper uniform – share some of the highlights that we have included in this book.[5]

A number of other individuals, more than can be named here, helped in their own ways towards the preparation of this book. However, the authors would be remiss not to mention the encouragement and support offered by Linda and Jim Buccini, Steven Franklin, Warren D.M. Reed, and John G. Kormann. Janice Wilson has provided expert editorial and research assistance throughout the project, and Jeanne Brandt helpfully scanned the images used in this book.

Curiously, it was an author of Civil War history, Jack Thomson, who spurred the initial preparation of this work into motion. Philip first encountered Jack as a tour guide on a Civil War Walking Tour in Charleston, South Carolina in April 2001. Later he renewed his acquaintance when Jack was signing copies of his work, <u>Charleston at War: The Photographic Record 1860-1865</u> at a Fourth of July author gathering that same year in Gettysburg sponsored by Greystone Communications and Greystone's American History Store.[6] Talking with Jack convinced Philip of what should have been obvious: to turn his historical skills towards recording his own father's history. As he noted in the copy of the book he signed for Philip, "Please try to record details of your father's World War II paratrooper service in Wesel, Germany, and <u>his</u> war." Thank you Jack Thomson for your gentle yet persuasive push!

Finally, two other helpful research tools must be acknowledged. The U.S. Army Military History Institute (USAMHI), part of the U.S. Army Heritage & Education Center (AHEC) in Carlisle, Pennsylvania, is conducting major survey projects to acquire first-hand source material from soldiers who served in World War II and Korea. Hopefully, the project will be extended in the near future for Vietnam veterans as well. This ongoing Veterans' Survey Project is truly helping to preserve the heritage of America's military for generations to come. Jointly

---

[5] Robert Wilson's military background was included in <u>War News: The Magazine of the Warfront and the Homefront</u>, Special Publication of the Mid Atlantic Air Museum's 13th Annual WW II Weekend, June 2004, p. 36. A more full account was shared with visitors that weekend in an eight-page pamphlet entitled, "Operation Varsity: 17th Airborne Crosses the Rhine March 24, 1945. One Participant's Perspective," © Robert L. Wilson and Philip K. Wilson, 2004.

[6] Jack Thomson, <u>Charleston at War: The Photographic Record 1860-1865</u> (Gettysburg: Thomas Publications, 2000).

completing this survey prompted Robert and Philip to more fully develop Robert's airborne activities. His completed survey, together with the completed surveys of several dozen other 17th Division WWII Airborne troopers, is available for public use in the holdings of the USAMHI.

Another excellent source of first-hand information from other WWII troopers who fought in Operation Varsity is "Thunder From Heaven," the Official News Bulletin of the 17th Airborne Division Association. Membership in this Association as well as subscription information for this twice-yearly publication is available from Edward J. Siergiej, P.O. Box 4793, Dowling Park, Florida 32064.

Chapter 1:

Parachutists: Military and Popular Perspectives

When people ask me what it feels like to jump out of a plane with a parachute, I say in all seriousness, "It's just like getting out of bed in the morning." You know how it is. Some mornings you hate to get up. Other times, when you have something important to do, you bound out with no thought of the hardships involved. Well, that's how it is with parachuting. It all depends on what's on your mind.

Colonel Edson D. Raff, Paratooper

Parachutists, now commonly called paratroopers, retain an active, important presence in U.S. military operations. The 22,000 members of the 101st Airborne Division (proudly boasting the moniker, "Screaming Eagles") were rapidly deployed on February 6, 2003 under the command of Major General David H. Petraeus as part of Operation Iraqi Freedom. They had recently participated in Operation Anaconda in Afghanistan, fighting to control the al Qaeda forces that were thought to be there in hiding. The 101st was also the only air assault force deployed during the Gulf War.[7] The 82nd Airborne Division (the "All Americans") has also actively aided war efforts to unearth *fedayeen* fighters in Samawah, north of Baghdad.[8] The use of these special airborne forces, however, is a relatively new tactic in the history of warfare.

Parachutes have been described for centuries. Although their design was discussed even earlier, Leonardo Da Vinci's drawing is typically credited as the first artwork representing a human suspended by a pyramid of cloth. He described that this apparatus, a tent of solid linen, would "enable a man to let himself fall from any great height without sustaining injury to himself."[9] Benjamin Franklin, America's own Da Vinci in terms of the manner in which he advanced new scientific and technological ideas, anticipated airborne warfare in 1787. Franklin's interest in air travel followed Pilâtre de Rozier's successful flight over Paris in 1783 in a hot air balloon designed by Joseph and Etienne Montgolfier. "Where is the Prince," Franklin quipped, "who can afford so to cover his country with troops for its defense, as that ten thousand men, descending from the clouds might not, in many places, do an infinite deal of mischief before a force could be brought together to repel them?"[10]

---

[7] Thomas Taylor, <u>Lightning in the Storm: The 101st Air Assault Division in the Gulf War</u> (New York: Hippocrene, 2003). The "Screaming Eagles" also presented a considerable force in Vietnam. See, for example, Keith William Nolan, <u>Ripcord: Screaming Eagles Under Siege, Vietnam 1970</u> (Novato, CA: Presidio Press, 2000). Tom Clancy provided an overview of recent U.S. Airborne forces in <u>Airborne: A Guided Tour of an Airborne Task Force</u> (New York: Diane Publishing Co., 1997). For brief Division histories, see W. Thomas Smith, Jr., <u>Alpha Bravo Delta Guide to American Airborne Forces</u> (NewYork: Alpha Books, 2004).

[8] Karl Zinsmeister, <u>Boots on the Ground: A Month with the 82nd Airborne in the Battle for Iraq</u> (New York: Truman Talley Books, 2003).

[9] <u>Establishment and Operation of a Parachute School in a Theater of Operations</u>, Prepared under the Direction of the Commandant (Ft. Benning, Georgia: The Parachute School, March 1943), p. 4.

[10] "Document on Joint Airborne Operations," (Ft. Bragg, N.C.: Joint Airborne Troop Board, June 18, 1954), cover.

Others including Simon de la Loubere, Fauste Veransio, Andre-Jacques Garnerin, Robert Cocking, and John Wise gained recognition over the course of the next three centuries for modifying designs and testing various types of chutes. Improvements in parachuting paralleled new designs in aerial ballooning. From the time of the U.S. Civil War when balloons were used for surveillance, parachute jumps from balloons became regular events at county fairs and political rallies. Civilian jumpers could even earn a living from this daring, though often short-lived, career.[11]

Following Orville and Wilbur Wright's success in conquering the air, parachuting gained new possibilities. However, the development of the airplane brought "new problems" to parachute design. A balloonist could jump from a damaged balloon, once his "dangers of remaining [in the balloon] overcame his fears of leaving," and descend in a harness tied to a single rope hanging from a vertical mounted aluminum tube on the outside the balloon's basket. The rigging lines and canopy of these parachutes – so called "Guardian Angels" – were deployed from this tube. In an airplane, however, the parachute itself "had to be small, without the big metal [externally placed] cylinder which served as a container for most balloon parachutes."[12] As air travel attained greater air speeds, stronger fabrics were required for chute design. And "gravest" of all, was the "danger of the jumper or his parachute getting tangled with the plane." Balloon jumpers knew that the moment they left their balloon, the balloon became significantly lighter and ascended, thereby not interfering with their own fall. However, those who made lifesaving jumps from disabled planes learned that the planes typically descend faster than opened parachutes. Many pilots, including Charles

[11] Among the more general overviews of parachuting in U.S. history, see Edwin P. Hoyt, <u>Airborne: A History of American Parachute Forces</u> (New York: Stein and Day, 1979) and E.M. Flanagan, Jr., <u>Airborne: A Combat History of American Airborne Forces</u> (New York: Presidio, 2002). However, Gerard M. Devlin's <u>Paratrooper: The Saga of U.S. Army and Marine Parachute and Glider Combat Troops during World War II</u> (New York: St. Martins, 1979) remains the cornerstone of U.S. trooper action in WW II. Interest in WW II U.S. Airborne activity remains strong, as evidenced by Williamson Murray's spectacularly illustrated overview, "Airborne Comes of Age," <u>World War II</u> 18 (2004): 26- 42.

[12] John Weeks, <u>Airborne Equipment: A History of Its Development</u> (New York: Hippocrene Books, 1976), p. 10.

Lindbergh, gained their initial parachuting experience by successfully diving from their plummeting planes. Others, however, were not so fortunate. Many pilots who had initially jumped clear of their plane and whose chute had opened successfully, were hit by their own plane as it circled around on its downward spiral. Thus, further modifications were necessary in order to develop a "manually operated" parachute that would only be opened after the jumper was "well removed from the vicinity of the plane."[13]

Not all parachutists from airplanes were pilots abandoning their disabled craft. On March 12, 1912, at Jefferson Barracks in Missouri, Captain Albert Berry made what was soon regarded as the first intentional parachute jump from a plane in flight. Other jumps followed, but it was the outbreak of the Great War (World War I) that accelerated the urgent need to produce safer airplane jumping. Initially, many military authorities were skeptical. They argued that carrying a parachute in a military plane would "encourage a pilot to leave his plane at the slightest danger." Indeed, they envisioned parachutes as promoting cowardice amongst their fighters. However, it soon became appreciated that "the replacement of pilots was much more difficult than the replacement of planes," and research and development efforts were hastened to "perfect a man-carrying parachute for airplane use."[14] Winston Churchill and Major (later Brigadier General) Billy Mitchell both foresaw great uses for parachute troops during the Great War.

By 1918, U.S. forces had developed two variations of the AEF (Air Experience Flight) parachute. The original model was made from cotton, and a later version composed of silk. However, the war ended before either version could be put to use. Following the war, further advances in parachute design were made at the Army Air Service Experimental Field Station at McCook Field, in Dayton, Ohio – the Wright Brothers' hometown. Based upon the work at this Station, orders were issued in March 1924 "requiring all Army and Navy fliers to wear parachutes."

Still, equipping special troops of soldiers with parachutes was slow to become a desired Armed Forces objective. In the U.S., a small group of volunteer soldiers gathered at Chanute Field, Illinois

---

[13] Establishment of a Parachute School, p. 5.
[14] Establishment of a Parachute School, p. 5.

in 1928. They successfully completed experimental jumps using the "free type" of parachute – a chute that was triggered to open merely by the weight of the descending jumper. Although their tests were successful, the concept of an "air army" was not taken seriously at the time; consequently, "the experiments received little attention." In the U.S., only the Forestry Service continued to experiment with improved designs. They envisioned using parachutes to successfully "drop fire fighters and fire fighting equipment in[to] inaccessible areas." Although they were fighting an enemy of fire, the Forestry Service's extensive work towards developing an apparatus for safer landings "proved of value to the Army" when the idea of forming parachute troops was eventually taken "in earnest."[15]

Before the U.S. military acted to form parachute troops, Russia and Germany had organized such units in their respective forces. Airborne efforts began in Moscow in 1930, and the Soviet Red Army established their Airlanding Corps in 1935.[16] German Luftwaffe developed an airborne regiment (*Fallschirmjägers*) that enhanced their existing strength in 1936. Within their forces, this regiment rapidly gained an elitism. This elitism of the *Fallschirmjägers* is evident from the "Ten Commandments" of the airborne fighters that they were required to commit to memory.

1. You are the chosen fighting men of the *Wehrmacht*. You will seek combat and train yourselves to endure all tests. To you the battle shall be fulfillment.

2. Cultivate true comradeship, for by the aid of your comrades you will conquer or die.

3. Beware of loose talk. Be incorruptible. Men act while women chatter. Chatter may bring you to the grave.

4. Be calm and thoughtful, strong and resolute. Valor and the offensive spirit will cause you to succeed in the attack.

5. The most precious thing when in contact with the enemy is ammunition. He who fires uselessly, merely to assure himself,

---

[15] Establishment of a Parachute School, p. 6.

[16] For a general history of Russian airborne efforts, see Charles J. Timmes, "Development of the Parachute and Airborne Activities in the U.S.S.R.," June 1952 typescript, U.S. Army Military Institute (USAMHI) of the U.S. Army Heritage & Education Center (AHEC), Carlisle, PA, hereafter refered to as USAMHI.

is a man of straw. He is a weakling who merits not the title of *Fallschirmjäger* (Paratrooper).

6. Never surrender. To you, death or victory must be a point of honor.
7. You can win only if your weapons are in good order. Ensure that you abide by this rule – first my weapon, and then myself.
8. You must grasp the full intention of every operation, so that if your leader is killed you can fulfill it yourself.
9. Against an open foe fight with chivalry, but to a guerrilla extend no quarter.
10. Keep your eyes wide open. Tune yourself to top condition. Be as agile as a greyhound, as tough as leather, as hard as Krupp steel: and so you shall be the German Warrior incarnate.[17]

Curiously, some German leaders critically challenged the usefulness of such airborne forces. Some two months after the German invasion of Crete on May 20, 1941 during which *Generaloberst* Karl Student, Commander of the German Airborne Forces, had led the first major airborne assault in history, Hitler strove to suppress further German airborne activity. "Of course, you know, General," Hitler told Student, "that we shall never do another airborne operation. Crete proved that the days of parachute troops are over. The parachute arm is one that relies entirely on surprise . . . . The surprise factor has exhausted itself."[18]

---

[17] Michael Hickey, <u>Out of the Sky: A History of Airborne Warfare</u>, (New York: Charles Scribner's Sons, 1979), pp. 21-22.

[18] Scott Garrett, "Airborne Through the Ages," in Bart Hagerman (ed) <u>U.S.A. Airborne 50th Anniversary, 1940-1990</u> (Paducah, KY: Turner Publishing Co, 1990), p. 34. For an overview of German paratrooper efforts, see Charles Whiting, <u>Hunters From the Sky: The German Parachute Corps 1940-1945</u> (New York: Stein and Day, 1974), Roger Edwards, <u>German Airborne Troops, 1936-45</u> (Garden City, NY: Double Day, 1974), Barrie Quarrie, <u>German Airborne Troops, 1939-45</u> (London: Osprey Publications, 1983), Chris McNab, <u>German Paratroopers: The History of the Fallschirmjäger in WWII</u> (St. Paul, MN: MBI Publishing Co., 2000), Christopher Ailsby, <u>Hitler's Sky Warriors: German Paratroopers in Action</u> (Staplehurst,UK: Spellmount Ltd, 2001), James Lucas, <u>Storming Eagles: German Airborne Forces in World War II</u> (London: Cassell, 2001), <u>Dominique François, The 508th Parachute Infantry Regiment: Red Devils: Normandy-Ardennes-Germany</u> (Bayeux, France: Editions Heimdal, 2003), as well as Robert Kurtz,

Germany's successful aerial invasion of Crete prompted airborne efforts in the United States. The recently formed 50th Transport Wing "scraped together a polyglot force of thirty-nine airplanes" and staged the U.S. Army's "first airdrop with more than one company of paratroopers in a single operation." These maneuvers, staged in Louisiana, revealed that the U.S. armed forces were "unprepared for modern war." "Much more was needed to be accomplished," and fears mounted in belief that "the time to do it was short."[19]

In July 1940, the U.S. War Department appointed two officers (Lieutenants William T. Ryder and James T. Bassett) and forty-eight enlisted men drawn from the 29th Infantry Regiment at Fort Benning, Georgia, a team known as the "Test Platoon" and operating under Major (later Major General) William C. Lee, to "conduct experimental jumps, with a view to organizing parachute troops in this country."[20] Their work culminated in the activation of the 501st Parachute Battalion at Fort Benning on September 16, 1940. At the time, it was thought that parachute troops would "seldom, if ever, be employed in units larger than a Battalion."[21]

German Paratroops: Uniforms, Insignia, and Equipment of the Fallschirmjäger in World War II (Atglen, PA: Schiffer, 2000). John G. Kormann compared the Crete invasion (Operation Merker) with that of the Rhine Crossing (Operation Varsity) in "Another View of Operation Varsity," The Airborne Quarterly 14 (2001): 12-13. For a more thorough coverage of parachute action in Crete, see Alan Clark, The Fall of Crete (London: Cassell, 2002), and the biographical memoir of one participating German paratrooper, Baron von der Heydte, Daedalus Returned (Littleton, CO: Aberdeen Books, 2001 reprint).

[19] Roger E.Bilstein, Airlift and Airborne Operations in World War II (Air Force History and Museums Program, U.S. Government Printing Office, 1988) p. 12.

[20] Establishment of a Parachute School, p. 6. John Weeks recounts the work of the Test Platoon in Airborne Equipment, pp. 36-40. For biographical information on Lee, see Jerry Autry, assisted by Kathryn Autry. General William C. Lee: Father of the Airborne: Just Plain Bill (San Francisco:, CA: Airborne Press, c. 1995).

[21] Organized Reserve Corps Airborne Training Course, Eighty Second Airborne Division, Fort Bragg, North Carolina (1941), p. 7.

Ft. Benning's Motto, "Drawn from the Skies," or "To March from the Skies"

The power and limitations of airborne units are identifiable through the range of mission objectives for which these forces were designed. These objectives included:

1) To seize, hold, or otherwise exploit important tactical localities in conjunction with, or pending the arrival of, other military or naval forces.

2) To attack the enemy rear and assist a breakthrough or landing by the main force.

3) To block or delay enemy reserves by capturing and holding critical terrain features, thereby isolating the immediate battlefield.

4) To capture enemy airfields.

5) To capture and destroy vital enemy establishments, thereby paralyzing his system of command, communications, and supply.

6) To create diversions.

7) To assist the tactical air force in delaying a retreating enemy until the main forces can destroy him.

8) To reinforce threatened or surrounded units.

9) To seize islands or areas which are not strongly held and which the enemy cannot easily reinforce.

10) To create confusion and disorder among the hostile military and civilian personnel.

11) As a constant threat by their presence in the theater of operations thereby causing the enemy to disperse his forces over a wide area in order to protect vital installations.[22]

Other descriptions of airborne troop objectives included spearheading invasions and assisting in breakthroughs as well as carrying out special missions of sabotage, intelligence gathering, guerilla actions, and rescue.[23]

The paratrooper, parachutist, "chutist", or "jumper" became an important new icon in the popular press, as heroes in action novels, and as the subject in myriad examples of artwork and music. Paratroopers graced the covers of popular magazines including Newsweek and the Saturday Evening Post. Life magazine's cover story of May 12, 1941 featured the U.S. Paratrooper. Following this feature article title, "U.S. Trains More Parachute Troops," we learn that "from 48 men last summer, [their] number will have increased to eight battalions of 4,048 men by Fall."[24] Although the reporter acknowledged that the *Fallschirmjägers* had served as the "model" for the U.S. troops, he

---

[22] Employment of Airborne and Troop Carrier Forces (Fort Leavenworth, Kansas: Command and General Staff School, 1944), p. 11.

[23] Lt. Col. Francis X. Bradley and Lt. Col. H. Glen Wood, Paratrooper (Harrisburg, PA: The Military Service Publishing Company, 1954), no pagination.

quickly noted that U.S. troopers were not "copying every detail of Nazi practice." For instance, it was speculated that the U.S. troops would not need a jumpmaster – the individual "whose job it is to see that all men actually jump." Rather, the U.S. troops will be "so highly trained" that they will "not have to be urged to jump."[25]

The Whitman Publication Company introduced paratroopers in their popular "Better Little Books" series. These works included Russell

---

[24] "U.S. Trains More Parachute Troops," Life (May 12, 1941), pp. 110-111. The U.S.M.C. also trained paratroopers at this time, but they abandoned airborne efforts in mid-1944.

[25] "U.S. Trains More Parachute Troops," p. 110.

R. Winterbotham's <u>Allen Pike of the Parachute Squad, U.S.A.</u> (1941) and Peter A. Wyckoff's <u>Uncle Sam's Sky Defenders</u> (1942). Whitman also introduced paratrooper Dick Donnelly in its young people's "Fighters For Freedom Series." Here, Dick Donnelly joins such figures as March Anson and Scoot Bailey of the U.S. Navy, Sparkes Ames and Mary Mason of the Ferry Command, Norma Kent of the WACS, Sally Scott of the WAVES, Barry Blake of the Flying Fortress, together with Nancy Dale, Army Nurse, and Kitty Carter, Canteen Girl – all of whom were caricatured as "red blooded Americans" who devoted their lives to "outfighting and outwitting a cunning enemy." As further enticement for potential readers of <u>Dick Donnelly of the Paratroops</u>, author Gregory Duncan revealed that Dick Donnelly "wasn't his [character's] real name and soldiering wasn't his profession." Rather, Donnelly volunteered for the paratroops because "he itched for excitement, action, [and] thrills" and, in Duncan's ultimate alluring line, because "it offered the quickest means of getting at the enemy with whom he had a personal score to battle."[26]

Paratroopers also hit the silver screen in director Leslie Goodwins' 1941 RKO Picture, "Parachute Battalion." This documentary styled war drama, co-written by John Twist and Hugh Fite, was thematically centered around the training of the 501st Infantry Battalion and used footage of actual jump scenes filmed at Ft. Benning. In "Parachute Battalion," the rigors of trooper training are viewed through the eyes of three young recruits: a football hero (Robert Preston), a colonel's son (Edmond O'Brien), and a hillbilly (Buddy Ebsen).[27]

---

[26] Gregory Duncan, <u>Dick Donnelly of the Paratroops</u> (Racine, WI: Whitman Publishing Co., 1944), inside front dust jacket.

[27] Harry Carey, Nancy Kelly, and Paul Kelly also had featured roles in this film.

Not all of the reporting on paratroopers was heroic and serious. Ced White, in an issue of Ft. Benning's newsletter, the "508th," wrote: "According to evolutionists, man developed into the following stages: 1) The Ape, 2) Pre-Historic Man, and 3) The Paratrooper. This, mind you, in spite of the fact that some scientists have declared a Paratrooper to be a throwback. Undaunted[,] the boys keep on jumping the same."[28]

---

[28] Ced White, "A Paratrooper," 508th, No 3. 1942. no pagination. "The 508th" Folder, William M. Miley Papers, Box 1, 1942, USAMHI.

Satires on the paratroopers also appeared in the comics of Bill Maudlin, Bill Yarborough, and George Baker's "Sad Sack" among others.

"It's best not to speak to paratroopers about saluting. They always ask where you got your jump boots."

In the music industry, Fred Waring and Jack Dolph enjoyed the success of their 1942 hit, "Look Out Below." Its lyrics celebrated that new fearless force of servicemen – the paratroopers.

When the guns are down and your silks flare out,
And the sky's full of guys that are tough;
When you know that spot they have picked is hot,
And the party's bound to be rough.

Do you wonder why you're a paraguy?
Why you dared to be scared? What the hell!
Oh, the answer's No! And it's Look Out Below,
For you'll go when you hear the man yell –
Stand up! Hook up! Go!

Look Out Below – Look Out Below
Let the old static line pull tight.
We're the toughest crew that ever flew
And we're swingin' down to fight.
Go Geronimo – Look Out Below!

Here we come in our domes of white
As we shout our war cry from the sky
Geronimo! Yeow! Look Out Below!
We'll be down in our domes of white
Shouting high our war cry from the sky

Geronimo! Yeow! Look Out Below!

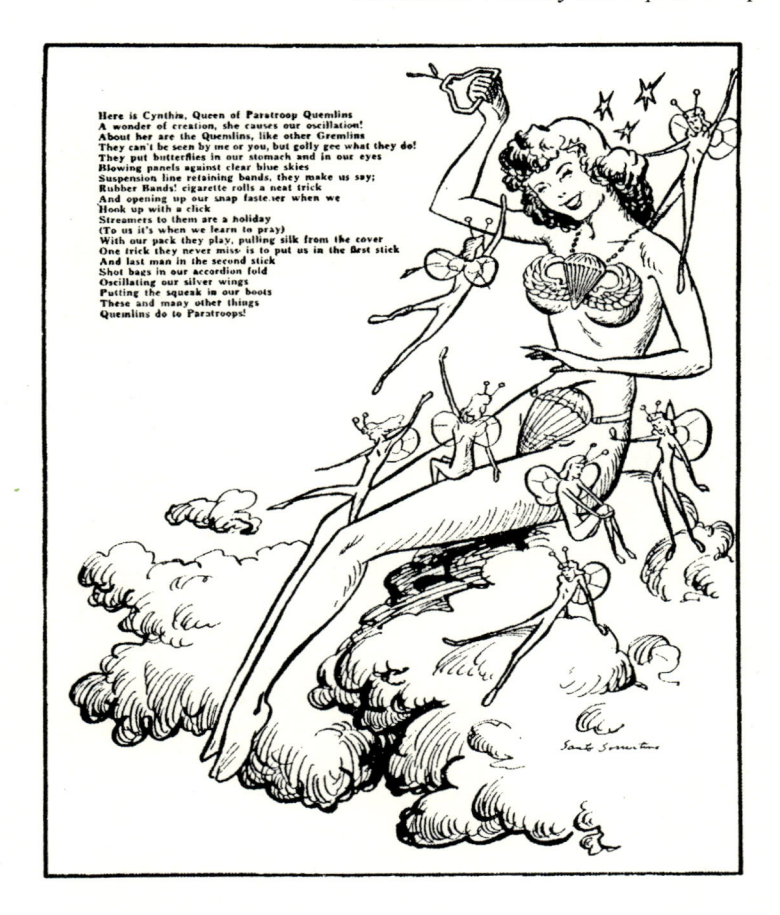

Even within the Army, the paratroopers gained legendary status. Their courage seemed invincible, and their arrogance as a "cocky bunch" soon became widely known. This invincibility came through in "The Paratroopers' Song," sung to tune of "The New Infantry March."

Oh, it used to be the Infantry
Did nothing but march all day;
These dusty guys, with mud in their eyes
Went slogging along their way.
But times have changed,
And now we range
The sea and the sky of blue to boot;
We fly a bit, and then we hit
The silk of a parachute, Oh . . . .

15

CHORUS

Airborne we fly the sky,
Paratroopers, do or die.
Ski troopers like the wind we go –
We're sons of guns, with tons of guns,
We won't take "No" for an answer.
Can't stop those paratroops
Thundering down into the fray.
Oh it's not the way it used to be –
A bigger and better Infantry
Comes in by air today.

The self-perceived invincibility of the troopers also came through the song, "Jumping Down to Victory," written to the tune of "Song of Burgundy":

We are the men in chutes,
Tough men in jumping boots,
Jumping down to victory –

We are the paratroopers!
Hard hitting parachuters
Jumping down to victory

Stand up, hook up:
Hit the door – and go!
Downward, earthward
Our silken banners flow

Lift up your heads
And shout it –
There's no doubt about it,
Jumping down to victory.
Geronimo!

CARTOON BY PARACHUTE CAPTAIN DEPICTS FAMILIAR SENSATION

Within the troops, they had their own playful songs as well, such as "Oh, How I Hate to Jump Out of an Airplane":

Oh, how I hate to jump out of an airplane!
Oh, how I'd love to remain on the ground!
For the hardest thing I know
Is to hear that man yell "GO!"
You gotta jump out; you gotta jump out;
You gotta jump out of the airplane.

Someday I'm going to murder the jumpmaster,
Someday they're gonna find him dead;
And then I'll get the other pup,
The guy that takes the airplane up,

And spend the rest of my life in bed.

Other aires addressed the hazardous duty associated with parachute jumping, using the morbid humor surrounding death that is often found in folk songs and ballads. One example, "Beautiful Streamer," was sung to the tune "Beautiful Dreamer."

Beautiful streamer, open for me,
Blue skies above me and no canopy;
Counted nine thousand, waited too long,
Reached for my rip cord, the darn thing was gone.

Beautiful streamer, why must it be?
While silk above me is all I should see
Just like my mother that looks over me;
To hell with the rip cord, 'twas not made for me.

Beautiful streamer, follow me down
Time is elapsing and here is the ground;
Six hundred feet and then I can tell
If I'll go to heaven or end up in hell.

Beautiful streamer, this is the end,
Gabriel is blowing, my body won't mend;
All you jump-happy sons of a gun,
Take this last warning as jumping's no fun.

Among all songs, the one that rang the loudest in the troopers's hearts and on their lips was their own theme song, "Blood on the Risers" sung to the national war tune, "Battle Hymn of the Republic." This tune was "dolefully sung over loudspeakers by a sad-voiced baritone" as "would-be troopers are marched off to their first jump" at Ft. Benning.[29]

He was just a rookie trooper and he surely shook with fright,
He checked all his equipment and made sure his pack was tight.
He had to sit and listen to those awful engines roar,
"You ain't gonna jump no more!"

CHORUS

---

[29] Bradley and Wood, <u>Paratrooper</u>, no pagination, modified slightly according to the version printed in <u>Paratroop Training</u> (Ft. Benning, GA, 1944).

Gory, Gory, What a Helluva way to die,
Gory, Gory, What a Helluva way to die,
Gory, Gory, What a Helluva way to die,
He ain't gonna jump no more!

"Is everybody happy?" cried the sergeant, looking up.
Our hero feebly answered "Yes," and then they stood him up;
He jumped into the icy blast, his static line unhooked,
And He ain't gonna jump no more!

CHORUS

He counted long, he counted loud, he waited for the shock,
He felt the wind, he felt the clouds, he felt the awful drop.
He jerked his cord, the silk spilled out and wrapped around his legs,
And He ain't gonna jump no more!

CHORUS

The risers swung around his neck, connectors cracked his dome,
Suspension lines were snarled and tied in knots around his skinny bones;
The canopy became his shroud; he hurtled to the ground.
And He ain't gonna jump no more!

CHORUS

The days he'd lived and loved and laughed kept running through his mind,
He thought about the girl back home, the one he'd left behind,
He thought about the medicos and wondered what they'd find,
And He ain't gonna jump no more!

CHORUS

The ambulance was on the spot, the jeeps were running wild,
The medics jumped and screamed with glee, rolled up their sleeves and smiled,
For it had been a week or more since last a 'Chute had failed,
And He ain't gonna jump no more!

CHORUS

He hit the ground, the sound was "splatt," his blood went spurting high,
His comrades then were heard to say: "A Helluva way to die!"
He lay there rolling round in the welter of his gore,
And He ain't gonna jump no more!

CHORUS

There was blood upon the risers, there were brains upon the Chute,
Intestines were a'dangling from his Paratrooper suit,
He was a mess; they picked him up, and poured him in his boots,
And He ain't gonna jump no more!

CHORUS

Chapter 2:
Airborne Attractions and Working for Wings

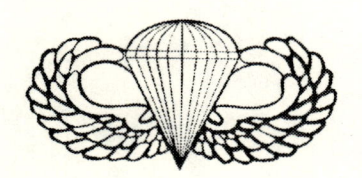

The training of airborne troops is no picnic but, on the other hand, there are few dull moments.

General William M. Miley, Paratrooper

"Greetings" came my way in a draft notice in December 1942, one year after the Japanese attack on Pearl Harbor. My family, then living in Elk City, Kansas, forwarded this notice, officially my "Order to Report for Induction," to me in Salinas, California where I was working at Spreckels Sugar Company. Just a year before, I had been working with my elder brother Tom as a riveter on the night shift at Consolidated Aircraft Corporation in San Diego, California. There, we helped Consolidated build their PBY Twin Engine Patrol Bomber Seaplanes. On reporting for work on the night of December 7, just after the Pearl Harbor attack, Consolidated enforced a "blackout" of all windows. The attack had urged us to work harder than ever. Among my first thoughts on learning of the attack were: "Where is Pearl Harbor?" and "I wonder what's next!" California did not seem to be the safest place in relation to its proximity to the outlying Hawaiian Islands.

Tom Wilson, U.S. Navy, WWII

My brother and I returned to our home in Kansas later that winter following the Pearl Harbor attack. A shell loading factory had just broken ground in Parsons, Kansas near Elk City in the southeastern part of the state. We joined other Elk City boys digging ditches before the factory's foundation could be laid. After hearing more about other fellows' experiences making better money on the West coast picking fruit, Pent Tharp, Grant Black, and I pooled our pocket money and bought a 1933 Plymouth. Our trip started out on a rough road, and while driving to Wichita, we had a blowout on a tire. We put on our spare tire but soon realized that no new tires were available as they were being rationed for war efforts. So, we traded the Plymouth even up for a 1929 Chevrolet that had new tires all the way around. Then, with our "California or Bust" attitude, we headed out the spring of 1942 for the west coast.

After several months of picking cherries, apples, peaches, and oranges in south central California, we had made very little money. So, we headed up northward to Salinas, an area rich with "truck farming," and there, we got a job hauling onions from the fields on a semi-trailer and transferring them into railroad cars. Although it was a good-paying job, we soon grew tired of the ever-present stench of onions and found another job – an inside job – at Spreckels Sugar Company. It was there, after several weeks of cutting sugar from the remnants of beets, that I received my "Greetings" that had been forwarded from Kansas.

Upon my hearing from Uncle Sam, we decided to drive back to Kansas together. I readily accepted my call to duty. Now, as a soldier, I could do even more to help protect and preserve our country. Overall, it seemed much more important and adventurous than what I had been doing with fruits and onions. I reported to the Draft Board in Elk City and asked to be placed in the Navy, as had my friend, Frank Foster. "Join the Navy and See the World" had been an attractive lure. However, for reasons unknown to me still, I was disqualified from Navy service. Perhaps it was merely because I could not swim. Overall, I was little bothered as there were still other ways to serve my country through Army efforts.

I received railroad tickets and an assignment to report to Leavenworth, Kansas. My mother, sisters, and younger brothers saw me off on the train as it left Elk City where I, together with two other local boys, Loren "Cotton" Welch and Alfred Black, left the farm for the fort. I was inducted into the service at Ft. Leavenworth in February 1943, the month of my twentieth birthday. Upon entering the service,

I felt ready to go to war. Still, I wondered greatly just what unit I would be assigned to and what they'll have me do. Where will they send me now? I'd just have to wait and see.

At that time, we knew that the war would not be ending soon. Having grown up on a farm, I had little idea of military life other than what a few school buddies who were already in the service as well as what my brother Tom, by then in the Navy, and another elder brother John, then in the Army, had mentioned in passing.

I was only at Ft. Leavenworth for a few days. While there, I received my shots, supplies, clothing, and a regulation style crew cut, then, after swearing my allegiance to serve only the United States, I boarded a train for boot camp. To our surprise, Cotton Welch, Alfred Black, and I had not been separated. Even more surprising, they were sending me back to California. I had received my draft notice while in California, drove home to Kansas, and was now being shipped back from Kansas to California. I wondered at the time "If I had just gone to the local California Draft Board, would I have ended up at the same place?"

We arrived at Camp Beale, California, some 10 miles east of Marysville and Yuba City, and an hour north of Sacramento. All of the time that I was in camp, it seemed to me that the sun rose from the west and set in the east. Outside of camp, my bearings were back to normal, but I never got used to the layout of the camp in directional terms. This was probably a good indication that I would not become a navigator.

Our first tactics of basic training were devoted to marching. Like many others, I had to overcome the fact that I did not have two left feet – although you would never have thought that from my initial days at marching drill. After learning the basics, we began unison marching. Then, we moved on to more precision marching, learning the Queen Anne's Salute – first using wooden dummy guns, and then our own rifles for this routine. It was comical to watch others, and I'm sure they got a kick out of me, too. Over time, we all somehow managed to master the basics of these close-order drills.

Despite many grueling stories that some report about their basic training, I truly enjoyed the experience. As farm boys, Cotton, Alfred, and I were pretty well prepared for this training, and we took it all in good stride. Together we figured out the ropes of military etiquette, marching and calisthenics, then moved on to the basic rules of riflery.

The three of us were assigned to the 273rd Field Artillery Battalion where some 500 soldiers were further divided into the mastery of machine guns, mortars, rifles, bazookas, canons, and explosives. We were assigned to the 105 howitzer (canon) Unit/Squad. Here, for about two months, we were drilled on the nomenclature of this piece of machinery and learned its purpose on the battlefield. We dismantled and reassembled this machine over and over as well as cleaned it again and again to ensure its proper working order as we fired live rounds on the artillery range. In simulating battle activity where no vehicle was available, we harnessed up and moved this machine, in teams of six or eight just like oxen, to the desired position. On our howitzer team, I carried and loaded ammunition as well as maneuvered the canon in harness.

Black and Welch, together with Bill Fox, a friend of ours from Wayside, Kansas, had been assigned to separate Batteries, but we still maintained close contact. To keep fit, we routinely headed off on distance marches and trained in guard duty. The cadences of practice guard duty, "Walk my post a mile a minute; An M-1 rifle and nothing in it," "Walk my post in a military manner, Obey the orders from the Company Commander," "Obey the orders I just received, from the son of a bitch I just relieved" still sing in my head – as do those with considerably more crude lyrics.

One day, out of the blue, I spotted a fellow who was wearing a paratrooper's uniform. It was quite distinguished looking compared to the khaki's and common fatigues that we all wore in the 273rd. Well, who is he? Why does he get to dress like that? Once this fellow got a few of us off duty soldiers together in a small group, it was then I learned that he was a recruiter for the parachute troops.

Welch, Black, and I were chumming around on the grounds when, one day in July, the recruiter started talking to us. We listened to his spiel, but we had no interest in joining the parachute troops and went about our separate ways, mentioning it only a time or two afterwards. At first, I wanted nothing to do with this service. A month later, we ran into this fellow again, as well as other recruiting paratroopers. This time, however, we listened a little more closely. Some of the points they mentioned seemed more interesting than they had been before, and they left us with something to think about. The three of us, Welch, Black, and I, talked more and more amongst ourselves about the parachute troops. Think of the adventures that being in the troops might offer. Think of the excitement that it might bring! And, if you finished jump school, you received an extra $50 per month hazardous duty pay – a sum that would double our monthly pay. Now, it was sounding better and better all the time.

After considerable conversation among the three of us, we decided "Why not give it a try?" Still, we gave a lot of thought to the one major obstacle we would have to overcome – How were we going to tell our parents? We decided collectively that we would not tell our parents about paratroop school at this time. Rather, we would just tell them that we were being transferred to Ft. Benning, Georgia. Only after we – or any of the three of us – made it through this jump school would we have to tell our folks.

We all met the physical qualifications; we were between 18 and 32 years old, not over 185 pounds or 72 inches tall. Distance vision without glasses was at least 20/40 in each eye. We were "venereal disease negative," had normal bones, joints, muscles and no previous chronic injuries. According to the proviso of Ft. Benning's qualifications for paratroopers, "Because of the high degree of risk associated with parachute jumping," all recruits were to be "strictly voluntary." Also, because the required frequent jumps from planes "may result in serious injury or death, . . . only unmarried men may volunteer."[30] It was also reported that paratroopers must have "a high I.Q."[31] Perhaps this is one of those areas in which a high I.Q. does not necessarily correlate to considerable common sense. Who with any common sense would volunteer to jump out of planes in situations that held such high risks?

Paratrooper Ross Carter has aptly summarized the lure that the troops held for us. His account reflects the hype that we heard in our recruitment lectures. "Men joined the paratroopers because they couldn't resist the awful thrill of risking their life in a parachute. They

---

[30] Barry Gregory, <u>United States Airborne Forces</u> (New York: Gallery Books, 1990), p. 20.

[31] "U.S. Trains More Parachute Troops," p. 110.

were drawn into the outfit as by a magnet and, once in, wouldn't have left it if they got a chance. Each man had a supreme faith in his ability to take care of himself whatever the odds. For this reason paratroopers were at times a quarrelsome lot because they could never believe that anybody could beat the hell out of them."

Every "level of society" was represented with in the troopers, Carter continued. "Senators' sons rubbed shoulders with ex-cowboys. Steel workers chummed up with tough guys from the city slums. Farm boys, millionaires' spoiled brats, white-collared men, factory workers, ex-convicts, jailbirds, and hoboes joined for the thrill and adventure of parachute jumping. And so the Army's largest collection of adventurous men congregated in the parachute troops."[32]

---

[32] Ross S. Carter, <u>Those Devils in Baggy Pants</u> (Canton, OH: Claymore Publishing, 1979 reprint of 1951 edition), p. vi. For decades, Carter's book has been required reading for new Airborne soldiers at Ft. Bragg, North Carolina.

After six months at Camp Beale, the three of us Kansas farm boys headed off on a train destined for Parachute School at Ft. Benning, Georgia and for all of the adventure that being paratroopers implied. We felt as if we were beginning to live out a dream.

Major General William M. Miley, without Helmet

Ft. Benning, the site of the 501st Parachute Battalion, had been organized in October 1940 and placed under the command of Major General William M. Miley. Miley, a West Point graduate of 1918, had been in Germany following WW I as part of the 1st Division of the Army of Occupation. Subsequent to his exceptional series of commands over the next twenty years, Miley was selected in 1940 to organize and command the first parachute unit ever activated in the U.S. Army. This unit, the 501st Parachute Infantry Battalion, was activated at Ft. Benning, Georgia on October 1, 1940. Under his leadership, the "doctrines, equipment, tactics, techniques of jumping and landing, esprit-de-corps, mottos and traditions" were established. In essence, he became the "Father of the American Parachutist."[33]

[33] Bart Hagerman, "General Miley and 'His' Division," The Airborne Quarterly 10 (1997): 21.

This training ground was situated along the Chattahoochee River, near the Alabama ferryboat landing, amidst considerable swampland. Recently promoted Lt. Colonel William C. Lee, later known as the "Father of U.S. Airborne Forces," had been assigned to "jump train each new parachute battalion the Army formed."[34] The Civilian Conservation Corps followed Lee's suggestion and cleared a large wooded, grassless tract of land for a "jump field" just south of Lawson Airfield. Nearby, the Army engineers created two "double-decker" wooden barracks facing each other with a large mess hall at the end of the street between them to serve soldiers in troop training. Latrines were placed at the other end of the street and a PX was also situated nearby. Troopers were the only group of Army men that ate as battalions rather than as companies in their respective mess halls.[35]

Although several groups of troopers had graduated from Parachute School by the time I arrived in August 1943, it was still a relatively new arm of Army service training. Our first glimpse of the School was the parachute towers which, as fellow paratrooper Kurt Gable described "dominate[d] the Fort Benning skyline" and offered a "grotesque welcoming committee to the Army's version of . . . [Dante's] Inferno."[36]

---

[34] G. M. Devlin, Paratrooper, p. 96.

[35] Kurt Gable, The Making of a Paratrooper: Airborne Training and Combat in World War II (Lawrence: University of Kansas Press, 1990), p. 93. For another interesting account of parachute school at Ft. Benning during WW II, see Francis L. Sampson's Look Out Below: A Story of the Airborne by a Paratrooper Padre (Washington, D.C.: Catholic University of America Press, 1948).

[36] Gable, Making of a Paratrooper, p. 35.

True to that vision, Parachute School was, up to that time, the roughest four weeks of my life. Commando training "may be tough," Marine boot camp may "bring blisters to your feet, your hands, and your soul – but the paratrooper's training course does all that and something more."[37] On top of all the physical demands, it was especially hot in

---

[37] Keith Ayling, <u>They Fly to Fight: The Story of Airborne Divisions</u> (New York: D. Appleton, 1944), p. 48.

Georgia in August. This was particularly the case in the "Frying Pan," that part of the camp where jump training occurred. To me, from the time I arrived at Ft. Benning until I got my wings, I felt as if I was always in a frying pan – truly in the fire. Our welcome, like the one Gable recounted, went something as follows: "You are in the Frying Pan, the reception station of the parachute school. No one asked you to come here. You will not be welcome until we decide that you are fit to become one of us."[38] In the words of a paratroop sergeant, "When we're through with you, you'll be as near to superman as any training can make you. You'll have to be. In our job, remember it is you or the enemy. We do not retreat. We drop on our objective, and we go forward to take it, or are dropped ourselves."[39] Our training course was mapped both to physically condition us for jumping and to "make habitual all the actions and skills needed in troop parachute jumping." As we would soon learn, the "training you will receive here is more strenuous than [that] in any other branch" of the service. We believed, as we were informed, that we were "a superior group of soldiers" who "want[ed] to be in Uncle Sam's best outfit."[40]

---

[38] Gable, <u>Making of a Paratrooper</u>, p. 37.
[39] Ayling, <u>They Fly to Fight</u>, pp. 2-3.
[40] <u>Establishment of a Parachute School</u>, p. 4.

Attaining and maintaining optimal physical endurance was emphasized throughout Parachute School. This was especially the case during the first week of classes that was devoted primarily to physical training. When we were not involved in other activities, we were always doing calisthenics. As much as anything else, we learned to do push-ups. Everywhere we went, we moved in double time. This was a significant change from the atmosphere at boot camp. A paratrooper in training never walked or stood still for any length of time. "He runs between instruction areas. If he wants to go to the latrine, he must run both ways. If he wants a drink of water he runs to the fountain and back."[41] At times, we had to run "over rough ground carrying about ninety pounds of equipment," to simulate the weight we would be carrying in combat.[42] "You're gonna double time until you are blue in the face – You can't quit – you can't lay down – so go ahead – fall on your face and they'll stand you up and run you some more."[43] If that did not work – "Step on top of him. Nobody Stops, you understand, Nobody?"[44] The only lying down we did was as night. Roused at 5:00 am and lights out at 8:30 pm, we never had difficulty falling asleep.

The other peculiar routine that we learned the first week was the "Jab." The Jab was unique to paratroopers and was used as a method to keep us alert. One trooper recalled that the jab was used to "trigger instant, unthinking responses."[45] No matter what you were doing, when an instructor called "Jab" you stood up and slammed your right fist to your upper left chest – and I mean slammed. You had to keep still in this position until the instructor called out "Recover." Only then could you drop your hand to its normal resting position. However, the instructor might call out "Jab" again before he called "Recover," in which case you slapped your left fist to your upper right chest, standing still and cross-armed. We could not "Recover" from this position until

---

[41] Bradley and Wood, <u>Paratrooper</u>, no pagination.

[42] Ayling, <u>They Fly to Fight</u>, p. 50.

[43] "To A Friend" letter in <u>Paratroop Training</u> (Ft. Benning, GA, 1944).

[44] John F. Magill, <u>We Led From The Sky: A Combat Paratrooper's Story</u> ('Computer Printed,' c. 1998), p. 5. WWII Veteran's Survey, "17th Airborne Division," Box, "Magill, John. F" Folder, USAMHI.

[45] Gabel, <u>Making of a Paratrooper</u>, p. 44.

ordered to do so, and the instructors often took advantage of this and talked to us at great length in our peculiar position of attention. After the first few times, the sound of the Jab in unison was quite impressive – it pierced the air like a loud rifle shot.

As in everything else, if we did not properly perform the Jab, we were punished with more pushups. Our sergeant, the Non Commissioned Officer (N.C.O.) in charge of our training, that white tee-shirted commando, held firm control. Pushups were punishment for just about anything – just for "leaning, sitting, or forgetting" during one of our hourly 10-minute breaks.[46] I got to the point where, when asked to "Drop and give me 75!," I would ask "Which hand?"

Unlike our boot camp experience, Parachute School N.C.O.s did everything right along with us. Indeed, they were so well conditioned that they grinned all throughout our exercise routines, making us feel all the more reluctant to moan and groan.

At the end of the first week of training, we all believed that we were in top physical condition. We felt as if we were truly on our way to becoming paratroopers. We lost around 30% of our classmates at this point due to their poor performance in the physical training.[47]

The "making of a paratrooper" was viewed by some to be a "studied scientific development."[48] Yet, part of that development involved prompt, effective, and complete medical care for any potential trooper wounded in training. In order to keep men in top physical condition, the Dispensary at Ft. Benning was considered to be such that "no other medical center beyond the walls of a hospital can boast such an array of equipment and technicians." In addition to treating a steady supply of soldiers with sprained muscles and broken bones in the large Physical Therapy Department, the Dispensary staff paid particular attention to our teeth. Teeth were "checked and rechecked, not only to insure their perfect condition but as a means of permanent identification." [49]

---

[46] Magill, We Led From The Sky, p. 5.

[47] One 1945 War Department report claimed that one-fourth of the men enrolled in the Parachute School fail and "approximately another fourth show up as 'weak' at some point in training." "Prediction of Success and Failure of Paratroopers Based on Background and Training Data," U.S. War Department. Troop Information and Education Division, 18 October 1945.

[48] Bradley and Wood, Paratrooper, no pagination.

[49] Ayling, The Fly to Fight, p. 46.

Each day for the next two weeks the course was divided into (parachute) Pack Training in the mornings and outdoor Jump Training in the afternoons. During the first of these weeks, jump training was an intensive, four-hour-per-day activity. This training was designed to give us "a complete knowledge of the technique of jumping" and to develop our "physical and mental capacities" such that each trooper "can cope with any situation that may arise during his jumping."[50] We were reminded that parachute jumping was "not unduly difficult," but that the jumper "must be thoroughly familiar with [all of] the characteristics of the descending parachute." He must "know how to check oscillation – that pendulum like swing of his body caused by rolling motion and the pressure of wind in the canopy." He must

[50] <u>Establishment of a Parachute School</u>, p. 6.

"know how to control the parachute in the air to avoid bumping into jumpers and how to avoid hazards on the ground such as stumps and telephone lines." He must "know how to turn his body in the air so as to come in on forward landings," and he must "learn to judge distances from the ground and to meet the ground with muscular readiness," landing neither stiff nor limp.[51]

Parachute jumpers "must be in excellent physical condition, not only to keep from getting hurt, but to meet the tactical situations that may arise after landing." The better the physical condition, the less likely the jumper will sprain muscles or break bones. Remember, our course instructors argued, that in tactical jumping, "an injured man is of no value. He is a detriment, in fact, for he may acquire the attention of another man."[52]

Physical conditioning during this week of jump training began with tumbling. Tumbling, according to our instructors, taught us "how to absorb the landing shock . . . when you hit the ground." Moreover, it will help you "regain your feet quickly, so that you can collapse your parachute and escape being dragged along the ground by a strong wind." Forward, rear, and zig-zag tumbles (first over right shoulder then over left) were drilled throughout the week.

Soon, we became persuaded to think more about our assigned mission than about ourselves. In order to "secure a position, or to aid ground forces in an attack, or to do any of the missions normally assigned . . . parachutists must be put down in very large numbers." Although we initially learned how to jump without hurting ourselves, we also knew that nearly all tactical jumps involved masses of jumpers, each exiting the plane one immediately after another. Thus, it became at least as important to know how to jump without hurting other jumpers. As one Parachute School story related, "Think of a transport plane flying about a hundred miles an hour over the jumping area. The first man jumps, then the second, third and fourth. But the fifth man hesitates. Maybe something has gone wrong with his equipment, because he didn't know how to take care of it, . . . [or] maybe he just loses his nerve. Then he collects himself and jumps, several seconds

---

[51] <u>Establishment of a Parachute School</u>, p. 6.
[52] <u>Establishment of a Parachute School</u>, p. 6.

later. The plane has traveled several . . . [miles] in this time, and the rest of the squad jumps with that much delay to handicap them. If the field is just big enough to hold a squad jumping in the normal time of about ten seconds for twelve men, the last four or five men will land off the field, maybe in trees, ditches, high tension lines—maybe even in the ocean. In combat they may get separated from the rest of the squad and never make contact, thus probably defeating the mission. So you can see your obligation to jump without hesitation."[53] That was a powerful mental message that drove a sense of responsibility into our minds.

Mock Up Door

---

[53] Establishment of a Parachute School, p. 7.

The first time that we began to feel that jump training was something more than intense boot camp was when we started jumping through Mock Up Doors. These doors resembled the cabin of the Douglass C-47 or C-53 planes from which we would eventually jump. These door exiting exercises taught us the proper method of inspecting equipment before jumping, allowed us to practice hooking up, and exposed us to the jumping commands: Stand Up and Hook Up; Sound off for equipment check. We worked in groups called a "stick" or "jump-stick," terms that troopers used to identify the group of men that jumped from one plane. After ensuring that the jumper in front of me, for example, the 6th man in the stick, had the release box of his harness closed and his parachute pack tied tight, I shouted out "Six O.K," then slapped him on the shoulder. He, in turn, checked the trooper in front of him. The orders, "Close Up," "Stand to Door," and finally, "Go," then followed in quick succession. The only difference in the jump from the Mock Up Doors, we were told, was the "absence of the prop-blast." [54] Of course, there was that difference in altitude. We were taught to stand at the door with the toe of our left boot over the edge of the door frame, with our right foot ten inches behind. Our knees were to be slightly bent, our back "crouched to an angle of about 45 degrees," and our hands placed outside each door about hip level, head and shoulders through the door exposed to the prop-blast, head up and eyes focused on the horizon.[55]

---

[54] Establishment of a Parachute School, p. 6.
[55] Establishment of a Parachute School, p. 15.

Jumping Out, WWII Memorial, Washington, D.C.

Upon hearing the command "Go," the jumper "shoves off with feet and hands both pushing, swinging his right foot forward and slightly to his left, thus facing toward the tail." His arms were to be crossed on his chest, with his right hand "on, but not clinching" the ripcord grip. His head should be bent forward, his body straight, and his feet together. We were encouraged to jump "with a very determined leap," for otherwise, we stood the risk of having the prop wash drag us all "along the [plane's] fuselage to the tail, causing painful burns to arms and legs."[56] They warned, if you dive head first, the chute opening will "snap you back up again by the shoulders, and you will get a jerk [just] like popping a whip." If a paratrooper exited sideways or backwards, we were informed that the parachute would snap us around. The worst that was likely to come of such mistakes, they argued, was that a paratrooper would "bruise . . . [his] shoulders a little and maybe [get] ... a crick in the neck." However, they drove home the message that we were expected to "learn to do it perfectly every time."[57]

In one area of our training camp, four-foot platforms had been built from which we learned to land on the balls of our feet, to time our landing by pulling on the risers, to follow our landing with a tumble, and to develop our leg and ankle muscles. We also learned to tuck in our elbows in order to reduce the risk of breaking our arms. Rope climbing was another big part of our jump preparation. "Can you climb a rope? Yea? Well, you just think you can. You'll climb a rope thirty feet high – your arms will cramp, your fingers will freeze – you can't possibly climb another foot; but they will drive you – and Brother – the men will make it, the boys will fall by the wayside."[58]

In another training area, we were placed in a suspended harness after having thoroughly reviewed the composition and actions of such a contraption and having learned the correct "landing attitude" in terms of physically meeting the ground. Our instructors drilled us on common parachutist's errors. We were shown why not to land on our heels, why not to land stiff legged, why not to lift or "bicycle" our legs as we approached the ground, why not to hold our feet at different levels or too far apart, and why not to let the downward pull affect our body positioning.[59] We also practiced body turns and "the slip," or pulling on the risers in the direction that you wish to descend, as well as controlling our oscillation all from within the suspended harness. By the end of our time in this apparatus, we knew why it had earned the moniker "ball breaker."

---

[56] Gregory, United States Airborne Forces, p. 33.
[57] Establishment of a Parachute School, p. 15.
[58] "To a Friend" letter in Paratroop Training (Ft. Benning, GA, 1944).
[59] Establishment of a Parachute School, p. 18.

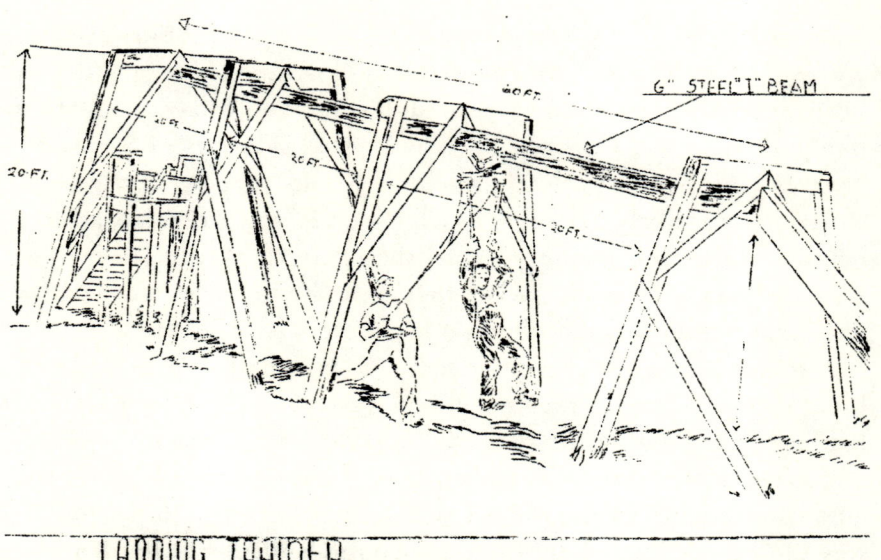

LANDING TRAINER

The second week of jump training (our third week of Parachute School) introduced us to a new series of apparatus. One of these was the Landing Trainer. Easier to view than to describe, this apparatus helped familiarize us with judging distances as we descended. We would first ease off the 10-foot high platform, "keeping one hand on the rail until clear, being careful not to touch the trip ropes." Then, upon command, we prepared to land – "feet on line, width of hips apart; knees slightly bent; toes slightly down; hips level; stomach drawn in; arms over head grasping risers; vision five to ten feet to the front."[60] The assistant running behind us along our descent tripped the rope, releasing us about a foot from the ground. This procedure taught us to break the landing shock by landing on the balls of our feet and enabling us to roll forward with momentum at the time of landing. Overall, it helped us master the parachute landing fall.

---

[60] Establishment of a Parachute School, p. 32.

Mock Up Tower

We also spent time each day of that week jumping from the Mock Up Tower. Lt. Colonel Lee had secured the idea of this tower from a German paratrooper training handbook. At the German parachute school in Stendal, near Berlin, troopers jumped through a Mock Door and tumbled down onto a mat positioned a few feet below. However, "to add more realism," Lee had the U.S. version of the Mock Up Tower positioned on the "highest supports they could find." Telephone poles were found nearby which, when "anchored into cement," rose "thirty-four feet high." [61]

From this 34-foot platform, we jumped in a harness secured to a two hundred foot steel suspension cable and descended towards a pile of sawdust below, all the while hanging on to our risers. The other end of our risers was attached to a metal wheel atop the suspension cable. These Mock Up Tower jumps taught us the proper technique of exiting a plane, the sensation of falling through space, and the shock of the chute opening as we hit the midpoint of the suspension cable. Designers of the Parachute School claimed "It's just as hard to jump from the tower as it is from the plane. A little harder, maybe, with the ground right below you instead of a long way down." After a few jumps from the tower, they concluded, "you need have no fear of freezing up when you go for [the] record in a plane jump." [62]

In reality, so many people froze on this apparatus that it became widely known as the 'Great Separator' – "more would-be troopers quit on the Mock Up Tower than in any other stage of jump training." [63] However, I thought this set up was great fun, and I took as many jumps from this Mock Up Tower as I could – some eight to ten in total. Overall, it seemed much safer than many of the leaps we had taken off of rooftops and out of trees on the farm. It also gave us further opportunity to make equipment checks on the soldier just in front of us in line. It is difficult to overemphasize the sense of security that we gained through equipment checks. This procedure, perhaps more than any other that we learned at Parachute School, helped to bond the members of a stick together in a sense of brotherhood.

---

[61] Devlin, <u>Paratrooper</u>, p. 97.
[62] <u>Establishment of a Parachute School</u>, p. 33.
[63] Bradley and Wood, <u>Paratrooper</u>, no pagination.

We also practiced parachute maneuvers from 250-foot towers. Lt. Colonel Lee, who had helped form the parachute troops, had, together with representatives of the Infantry Board, "witnessed controlled parachute jumps" made from the Pair-O-Chutes towers at Coney Island's Steeplechase Park during the World's Fair in New York on July 7, 1940. "Impressed with these demonstrations," Lee recommended that the Parachute Test Platoon be "moved to Hightstown, New Jersey, for a week's training on two 125-foot towers at the Safe Parachute Company."[64] In due course, four 250-foot towers were built at Ft. Benning.

We made our first parachute descents from these 250-foot towers. Some of these were controlled descents whereas others were complete release drops. Four trainees at a time could be descending from these towers as one chute was attached to each of the ends of two cross beams atop the tower. However, we typically did not use the arm that extended in the direction from which the wind was blowing. A trainee dropping from that arm would likely have crashed into the central support merely from the gusts of wind. But even from the other arms, when the wind blew, as it often did, we quickly learned to perfect "the slip" procedure in order to avoid crashing into the steel tower.

In these parachute descents, we got to ride "on the 'buddy-seat' first." As paratrooper Kurt Gable noted, "That's the device you had to pay a lot of money to get a ride on at the World's Fair, and here you get it for free. We haul you up just to give you an idea of height. We haul you up a second time in a harness, and again you experience a controlled descent. The third tower [fall] is a 'free' tower [fall]. This one counts. You are attached to a thirty-eight-foot canopy and the only thing controlling your descent is you. Then you'd better do what you've learned during your manipulation training because you're on your own."[65] As I recall, we made eight to ten jumps from these towers, most of them during the daytime and at least one at night.

As one resource stated, "The jumper doesn't necessarily 'have it made' just because he has hit the ground. He may have to battle the elements even upon landing."[66] Controlling a parachute in wind gusts

---

[64] Gregory, <u>United States Airborne Forces</u>, p. 21

[65] Gable, <u>Making of a Paratrooper</u>, pp. 84-85.

[66] Bradley and Wood, <u>Paratrooper</u>, no pagination.

after landing has been compared to reigning in a team of runaway horses. To simulate such situations, in other training exercises we were laid down on the ground and attached to a chute that was partially inflated by a wind machine. When the instructors revved up this machine, the blow turned us into "a human sled." We learned how to recover from this position, get up quickly and collapse the chute, thereby minimizing this rough ride.

During the first of our two weeks of parachute pack training, we had seemingly endless lectures on the construction and operation of the parachute, the causes of and ways to remove twists and tangles, as well as lectures on panel folding and line towing. It was here that we learned everything about the standard T-7 assembly troop-type parachute, the lifting surface of the parachute (the twenty-eight foot canopy), its framework of suspension lines each with a tensile strength of 450 pounds, and the peculiar system of sewing lengthwise threads of fabric to confine any tears to individual sections of line groupings. The harness, that swing or saddle that attaches the canopy to the paratrooper, was demonstrated as was the pack that carried the main canopy on the back and the reserve canopy across the chest. Paratrooper Gable offers a telling glimpse into a typical lecturer's delivery of this information. "This is a T-7 parachute . . . . the apex . . . . the canopy . . . . the skirt . . . . a panel." There are "twenty-eight panels in a T-7, troop-type parachute, each twelve inches at the skirt. That gives you a twenty-eight-foot canopy." "Suspensions lines . . . . Civilians call these 'shroud lines.' If you ever call them that, you will do twenty-five push ups. They are suspension lines."[67] These lecture drills were always followed by review – and punishment for failure of recall – and written examinations for everyone at the end of each week.

In practical work sessions, we also learned in detail the intricacies of parachute inspection. Throughout these sessions, the mantra was

[67] Gable, <u>Making of a Paratrooper</u>, p. 85.

repeated that "A Parachute is as safe as the Inspection made upon it."[68] It was impressed upon us that "an inspection must be made before every repacking of the parachute."[69] The "finding of a weakened seam," it was argued, "is your added insurance."[70] We quickly learned that perfecting our ability of chute inspection was a heavy personal responsibility. "When you sign an inspection slip" at the completion of an inspection, "you are certifying that there is absolutely nothing wrong with that parachute."[71]

---

[68] Establishment of a Parachute School, p. 14.
[69] Establishment of a Parachute School, p. 15.
[70] Establishment of a Parachute School, p. 41.
[71] Establishment of a Parachute School, p. 41.

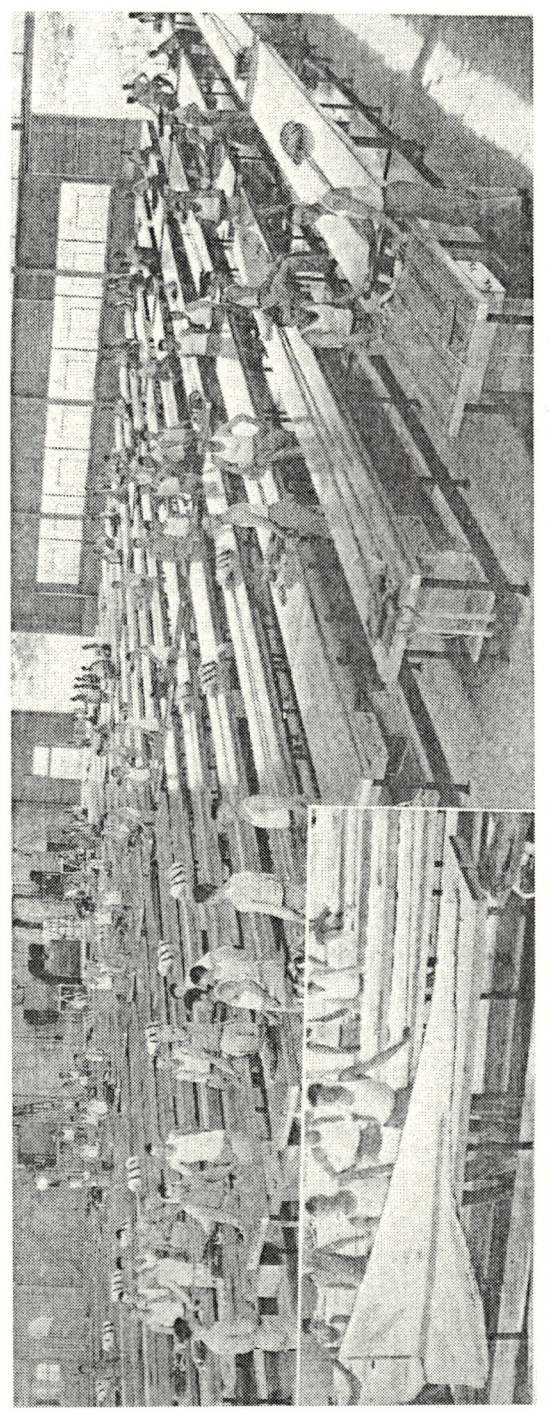

Panel Folding in Chute Packing Room

Panel folding comprised more than half of this first week's sessions, thereby attesting to the importance that the Army placed upon this procedure. The second week continued with more panel folding as well as learning how to create accordion folds in the canopy, tying the breakcord, closing the pack, stowing the static line (that fifteen foot of cotton webbing that attaches to the pack cover, the breakcord attaching loop, and, at the other end, terminates in the anchor line snap fastener that will ultimately be attached to the anchor line in the plane), as well as possible adjustments that could be made from within our harness. We worked on long white wooden tables whose surfaces were "specifically smoothed to prevent tearing or ripping of the precious [silk] fabric."[72] Some of our lecture sessions were devoted to using our reserve chute, whereas in others we learned about landing over forests, around high tension wires, and in water, and still others to special considerations that must be undertaken before night jumps. By the end of this week, we could pack a chute in about two hours. The last two days of the week were devoted to packing for our initial jump.

During our tactical training on parachute packing, we were ever conscious of chute care. We learned that we were responsible for packing our own chutes, thus we became even more alert of making every fold correctly. Parachute packing had to be just right because, in the end, it is my chute and my jump. We had to depend upon our own work. It was a slow process getting it just right, and if one had any inkling that he hadn't packed it just right, he'd do it all over again. Like instructors everywhere else in the Army, the Pack Training instructors wanted everything under their care to be just right. However, unlike the cadre of instructors who oversaw drills on the parade grounds, the Pack Training instructors were considerably more patient and helpful when we had individual questions.

At the close of these two weeks, we could rattle off the following sequence of events in our sleep: rise from seat, take anchor line snap fastener in left hand, break the holding cord of left shoulder adapter, snap fastener to anchor cable, shuffle to door, jump on command, 15-feet of static line plays out, lacing cord breaks, parachute pack's cover comes off, canopy pulls out, suspension lines pull out of restraining

---

[72] Ayling, <u>They Fly to Fight</u>, p. 55.

bands, tacking of risers breaks, air rushes up channel in silk as canopy inflates, break cord breaks due to the weight of the jumper, pack cover and static line stay with the plane whereas the remainder of the assembly accompanies the jumper. Should any of the above fail, then the reserve parachute – the trooper's "Best friend" – will be deployed. Now we were to put that training into real practice.

The final of our four weeks of Parachute School was devoted to actual jumps together with continuing our physical conditioning through calisthenics, running and walking exercises, obstacle course drill, and group games. Just as we did in everything else here at Parachute School, we had to cover the obstacle course in double time.

One jump was schedule for each of five days of this six day work week, with the sixth day reserved for graduation and assignment of duty as well as making up any required jumps that had been missed due to inclement weather earlier in the week. Wind gusts of over ten miles per hour, low cloud ceilings, visibility under three miles as well as rain, snow or excessive coldness were indications to cancel jumps for the day.[73]

On the Saturday of our third week at Ft. Benning, we finished packing the parachute that we would use for our initial jump on the following Monday. We signed into a log book the number of the chute that we had packed, and we knew that that very chute would be strapped on our back in just two days. Sunday, a day to ourselves, gave us time for quiet reflection – perhaps too much time on this particular Sunday.

Come Monday, clad in our regular fatigues, we picked up our chutes from the rigging room and checked our chute number against the log book. Getting into the harness and adjusting all of the straps just right took several hours – and our jitters on that particular day added even more time to this procedure. As Arthur W. Ferguson recounted about the time before his first jump in 1942, "I smoked numerous cigarettes, went to the water cooler a dozen times, adjusted my harness again, [and] looked to see if all the snaps were fastened. I forced myself to think about all the things my instructor had told me, and remembered that the percentages of casualties had been small.

---

[73] Establishment of a Parachute School, p. 39.

But a small thought would come creeping in, would I be one of those 'few casualties'?"[74] "Yea' – they'll tell you it 'always opens' – yea' – well, listen Jack – I've seen 'em ride a streamer down – all the way down – screaming until they hit with a deadening thump – did you ever throw a dead cow off the back of your wagon? Know that sound? Well – you might hear it – you'll never feel it. That's a good way to look at it Bud – if you hit hard enough – you'll never feel it." Those lines of graveyard humor, supposed lines of 'comfort,' were provided in our own <u>Paratroop Training</u> manual.[75] Troop plane pilots offered more light-hearted ribbing, claiming that they know of only two things that fell from the sky – paratroopers and bird shit. Indeed, our pilots never really appreciated the motivations of the troopers. They claimed that if their plane was in trouble, they were more inclined to "ride her down" than to jump out.

After properly placing our straps so as to distribute the shock of the opening parachute equally over the body, we boarded a truck and were transported to the airport at Lawson Airfield nearby. There, in the "sweat shed," we awaited our turn to emplane, hunched over from the tight strapping of the parachute pack, sweating from the heat and even more from the anxiety of the unknown that lay before us that day. I saw a number of other boys jump from their planes over one of the two drop zones (DZs), watching their hemispheres of silk open for them before my turn came up that afternoon.

I had seen airplanes, especially crop dusters before, but I had never seen one so close up. As this was going to be my first plane ride, I really thought that they could have at least familiarized us with flying in a plane, giving us a roundtrip ride before they made us jump out of one. But this is the Army, and they are all about efficiency.

---

[74] Arthur W. Ferguson, <u>Jump Happy</u> (New York: Privately Printed, 1942), p. 4.
[75] "To a Friend" Letter in <u>Paratroop Training</u> (Ft. Benning, GA, 1944).

C-47 Gooney Bird

At Lawson Airfield, we boarded our C-47 plane, the Curtiss plane commonly known as the "Skytrain" or "Gooney Bird" (or "Dakota" by the Brits) – the plane that had become the "Workhorse" of the Airborne. These low-winged monoplanes, the military version of the civilian DC-3, had a 6,000 lb payload capacity, twin Pratt and Whitney radial engines of 1200 hp each, and wings and engines composed of a "partially stressed aluminum skin."[76] They flew at a top speed of 220 mph and reached a maximum flight range of 1500 miles.[77] The planes had one door on the port (left) side of the fuselage just forward of the tail, leaving an open door way through which we entered and would later exit. These planes, as General Eisenhower later argued, were one of the four things responsible for the U.S. victory in World War II.[78]

---

[76] J. Weeks, Airborne Equipment, p. 103.
[77] Bilstein, Airlift and Airborne Operations in World War II, p. 16.
[78] The other three being the bazooka, the Jeep, and the atom bomb, as cited by Bilstein, Airlift and Airborne Operations in World War II, p. 17.

Oscar

There were twelve of us in our stick, together with our Jumpmaster. The plane took off, gained altitude, and we flew up to 1500 feet. Smoke signals on the ground marked the designated DZ. "Oscar," our "dummy paratrooper" was thrown from the plane to ensure that the wind was not too strong for us to deplane. As the pilot approached the tree-cleared DZ, the red light came on, indicating our need to get prepared. The Jumpmaster shouted "Stand Up," "Hook Up," "Check Equipment," "Shuffle to the Door." We had to shuffle so as not to cross our feet or trip as we approached the door. While shuffling, we kept our balance by holding on to the cable or the static line.

Tension ran high among those in our stick. "Is everybody happy?," roared the Jumpmaster. This remark, as Gable noted, was "supposed" to "relieve the tension," but it hardly did the trick.[79] When the green light came on, our stick started jumping at the Jumpmaster's command – a tap on the leg or butt. It is often remarked that if one hesitated, he'd soon feel the jumpmaster boot him in the ass right out the door. However, official documentation strongly encouraged jumpmasters to do all that they could to help each soldier make that first jump on his own volition. Officially, soldiers were not forced to jump, and indeed, a few did not make that first jump. However, among the troops, it was often joked, "Well, did you jump on your own or were you booted out?" Just where reality met official Jumpmaster guidelines remains known only to those who crossed through the door.

As I approached the door, midway in my stick, I was thinking "What the Hell am I doing here?" But then I remembered, "I know, its $50 extra a month – let's do it!" And I did. When I reached the door, I looked out and the blast from the propeller wrinkled my skin. Then, as I bent over looking down, pushing from the outside of the plane against the door frame, I got a tap from the Jumpmaster. However, unlike what I had been taught, I did not jump, but tumbled headfirst.

---

[79] Gable, <u>Making of a Paratrooper</u>, p. 116.

Out I went and completed my count, one-thousand, two-thousand, three-thousand. About the time my head reached my feet, my chute opened. That chute, typically creating a shock of 4 "G's," really jerked me around, turning me every which way but loose. But when I looked up and saw that big round piece of silk holding me up – Oh! Was that beautiful. The next ninety seconds in the air (what we called "hang time") felt like Heavenly bliss. One paratrooper in training described this part of his jump as being ever so quiet, "just like it is when snow is falling on a cold winter night."[80]

My chute popped open, and I was swinging back and forth like a pendulum on a clock. I was really feeling great and so glad that I had packed my chute right. Indeed, there were no reports that anyone's chute had malfunctioned during our first day of jumping. A few instances of someone landing in another's chute did occur, but they got untangled before collapsing their chutes.

Now that my chute had opened, I had to think about the landing. Landing, after all, was the most dangerous part. As it is for airplanes, the ground is the paratrooper's worst enemy – at least during training sessions. If you had paid attention to what the instructors had tried to teach you, then you had good chance of not getting hurt – at least not too badly. All of these instructions were running through my head – remember how to land, tumble, and roll. Still, had we completely forgotten what to do, we could rely upon the instructors who were coaching us down (literally shouting at us) through their megaphones from the ground below. My first landing was good. I had no trouble coming down correctly and gathering my chute. I guess that my experience was better than that of General Ridgway who described his first landing as "about like jumping off the top of a freight train, traveling at thirty-five miles an hour, onto a hard clay roadbed."[81]

Once on the ground, I now had to pick myself up, get out of my harness, and pull the bottom cords of my chute towards me, "spilling" the chute, causing it to collapse, and then wadding it up into a huge armful of silk and cords. If the wind would have been strong, I would

---

[80] Ferguson, <u>Jump Happy</u>, p. 6.
[81] Matthew B. Ridgway, <u>Soldier: The Memoirs of Matthew B. Ridgway</u>, as cited by B. Gregory, <u>United States Airborne Forces</u>, p. 30.

have needed to gather my chute before releasing myself from the harness. However, I was not bothered by the wind on this jump, and I gathered my chute in without any problems. I then headed for the "6x6" truck, running double time of course, to be returned to the packing shed.

On route, we were really a joyful bunch of guys, slapping backs and shaking hands as we congratulated each other on having successfully completed our first jumps. Still, time for celebration was short, for when we arrived at the packing shed, we had to pack our chutes for the next day's jump. We hoisted our chutes up, stretching them out on the rigging towers in the sheds, from which we could get all of the weed stems and sand burrs removed. Then, we laid our chutes out on the rigging tables to brush the dirt off. The days were hot and dry in Georgia at that time of year, therefore we avoided the additional cleanup problems caused from getting one's chute wet and muddy. As we cleaned our chutes on this particular day, everyone was in a cheery and congratulatory mood. Although we knew that many others had made similar jumps, for us, this was – and always would be – the time of celebrating our first jump. I was in a great mood, but like everyone else, I worked methodically to properly refold my chute and placed it into my backpack to be ready for tomorrow's jump. After all, I still had to achieve four more jumps before receiving my wings.

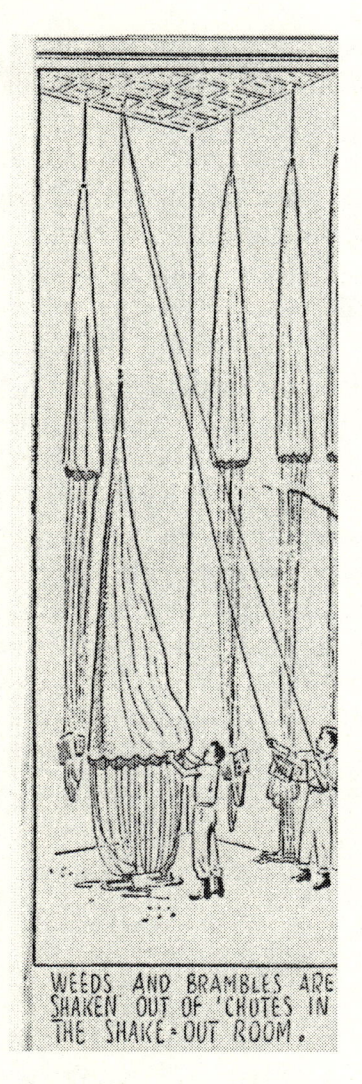

WEEDS AND BRAMBLES ARE SHAKEN OUT OF 'CHUTES IN THE SHAKE-OUT ROOM.

The supervisors at the Parachute School knew that they were asking men to act against nature. "A man's not normal if he's not afraid of his first few jumps. The idea is to jump anyway with all your instincts yelling at you <u>not</u> to jump. . . . You'll probably never get to the point where popping out of a plane is like walking through a door, but . . . it will get easier and easier all the time."[82] Indeed, everyone seemed much more relaxed during our later jumps.

----

[82] <u>Establishment of a Parachute School</u>, p. 8.

One point of a later jump that I remember vividly is watching the treetops – they came into view so very quickly as we fell through the air, and I knew that I was really falling fast. The pendulum swing was really hard to work through, and it took much practice in our future jumps to pull the risers in just the right way to properly manage my chute. The pilots dropped us from sequentially lower altitudes, ultimately simulating the actual distance from which we should expect to be dropped into combat. Our last jump was made from between 800 and 1000 feet.

Paratrooper Robert L. Wilson

After our fifth jump, we were now paratroopers, or as our certificate stated, qualified parachutists. There are "only two grades in this school: Superior – or Failure."[83] We who received the "Superior" grade were awarded our wings and our boots at the ceremonies concluding Parachute School. We were told to wear them proudly and to remember that we were a "cocky bunch" of men. I did my best to keep up this tradition. I would not have changed to any other branch of service even if I could have. Being "Airborne" was actually an attitude; a state of mind. Ft. Benning was our *alma mater*, the only one that I would ever have, and it was a "university of supermen."[84] As paratroopers, we considered ourselves in a league of our own, separate from and better than any other type of fighter in the armed services. Our extra pay reinforced this point as well.

In my heart, I fully ascribed to "The Parachutist's Creed":

I volunteered as a parachutist, fully realizing the hazards of my chosen service – and by my thoughts and by my actions will always uphold the prestige, honor, and high esprit-de-corps of the only volunteer branch of the Army.

I realize that a parachutist is not merely a soldier who arrives by parachute to fight, but is an elite shocktrooper and that his country expects him to march farther and faster, to fight harder, to be more self-reliant and to soldier better than any other soldier. Parachutists of all allied armies belong to this great brotherhood.

I shall never fail my fellow comrades by shirking any duty or training, but will always keep myself mentally and physically fit and shoulder my full share of the task, whatever it may be.

I shall always accord my superiors fullest loyalty and I will always bear in mind the sacred trust that I have in the lives of the men I will lead into battle.

---

[83] Bradley and Wood, <u>Paratrooper</u>, no pagination.
[84] Ayling, <u>They Fly to Fight</u>, p. 51.

I shall show other soldiers by my military courtesy to my superior officers and non-commissioned officers, by my neatness of dress, by my care of my weapons and equipment that I am a picked and well trained soldier.

I shall endeavor always by my soldierly appearance, military bearing and behavior, to reflect the high standards of training and morale of parachute troops.

I shall respect the abilities of my enemies, I will fight fairly and with all my might. Surrender is not in my creed.

I shall display a higher degree of initiative than is required of the other troops and will fight on to my objective and mission, though I be the lone survivor.

I shall prove my ability as a fighting man against the enemy on the field of battle, not by quarreling with my comrades in arms or by bragging about my deeds, thus needlessly arousing jealousy and resentment against parachute troops.

I shall always realize that battles are won by an army fighting as a team, that I fight and blaze the path into battle for others to follow and to carry the battle on.

I belong to the finest fighting unit in the Army. By my appearance, actions, and battlefield deeds alone, I speak for my fighting ability. I will strive to uphold the honor and prestige of my outfit, making my country proud of me and of the unit to which I belong.[85]

---

[85] William B. Breuer Collection, Box 2, "Material on the 517th Parachute Infantry Regimental Combat Team Campaigns in Southern and Central France," Folder, USAMHI.

Our paratrooper uniform was critically important to our image. In particular, we liked to show off our shiny wings and our shiny boots. "No matter what happened from then on, no one could take [our wings] away."[86] Our brevet of an eagle's wings extending from the sides of a parachute was designed by Lt. William P. Yarborough.[87] General Miley had wished to distinguish his troopers beyond a standard certificate, and he had assigned Yarborough to this task in 1941.

---

[86] Gregory, <u>United States Airborne Forces</u>, p. 33. Like many other troopers, I later paid a friend in the Motor Pool to solder an extra set of wings that I had purchased in the PX onto the flat shiny surface of my belt buckle, thereby adding another distinguishing touch to my uniform.

[87] Gregory, <u>United States Airborne Forces</u>, pp. 23-24.

Our boots, with their reinforced ankles and tops, stood out even more as we in the troops were allowed to tuck our pant legs into our boots, blousing them out over the top. Whenever we could find the time, we proudly polished our boots to give them an extra glistening, and we wore them with their laces precisely tied. Yarborough had also designed these boots, replacing the buckle and strap of the GI infantry boot with heavy duty stitching and laces. This configuration of the troopers' boots was a safety measure as it prevented them from becoming entangled with the rigging lines like an unbuckled strap had sometimes done. Furthermore, when laced tightly, they strengthened our instep in order to prevent injuring our feet upon landing. The metal toe cover provided additional protection.[88]

To reinforce the importance of boots to a paratrooper, let me relate a story from Robert Flory of the 101st Airborne Division. In early spring of 1944, two battalions of the 506th Parachute Infantry Regiment stationed in Britain were called upon to perform a practice jump "to impress a delegation of V.I.P.s" including Prime Minister Winston Churchill, Supreme Commander Dwight D. Eisenhower, and Major General Maxwell D. Taylor, the Commander of the 101st Airborne. "At the prejump briefing the troops were instructed to camouflage themselves on the drop zone immediately after landing." Two troopers landed in a large field, "devoid of any possible covers, except for a large hay stack at the edge of the road. They decided to bury themselves in the hay and take cover from a light rain that was starting to fall. . . . Not long afterwards a staff car came up the road and stopped alongside them." In the car were Churchill, Taylor, and Eisenhower. "Churchill gets out, walks over to the hay stack and starts pissin' all over my boots." The trooper later asked, "do you think I should have shot him? I don't care if he's the Prime Minister or not, I don't want him pissin' on [my boots]!"[89]

When I joined the troops in 1943, we were the only special section of the Army that was allowed to dress in this manner, and the insignia of the paratrooper was "the most coveted and honored in the Army."[90] Some troopers had the image of their wings tattooed on their chests,

[88] Gregory, United States Airborne Forces, p. 24.
[89] Robert A. Flory, "Churchill's Secret," Airborne Quarterly 9 (1996): 7.
[90] Bradley and Wood, Paratrooper, no pagination.

others wore their actual wings on their sleepwear. And, as the story goes, an "airborne bride must get used to the fact that her husband will wear his boots and emblems at all times."[91]

Paratrooper Robert L. Wilson

[91] Bradley and Wood, <u>Paratrooper</u>, no pagination.

Airborne troopers were also identifiable by a patch on their overseas cap. So "highly prized is this insignia" that troopers had "special permission to wear the overseas cap when off-duty instead of the visored cap which is required to be worn by [all] 'straight legs'" – the non-airborne soldiers.[92] For further distinction between troopers, artillery men wore a white parachute on their red oval sidecap patch whereas the infantrymen wore a white parachute on a blue patch. To help our wings stand out upon our olive-colored uniform, we wore them over a regimental colored background patch. When wearing pith helmets, our reinforced chin strap or cup with leather lining further distinguished our appearance from that of the "straight-leg" GIs. Troopers "invariably released the chin cups immediately after landing and left it swinging beside their faces." As such, it "quickly became one of the airborne soldier's trademarks."[93]

Upon completing Parachute School and having received our wings, marched in a Wing's Parade, and enjoyed a Prop Blast Party, our assignments were posted. Black got sent to the 101st Airborne Division in Ft. Campbell, Kentucky, Welch received a furlough, and I was sent to North Carolina. Now was the time, as we had previously agreed, that we would tell our parents that their sons were paratroopers. Welch's parents raised so much hell with him that when he reported back to Ft. Benning, he refused any further parachute jumps and was sent into a non-airborne unit. My parents, together with those of Black, went along with our decisions. At that time I signed over a bond so that $17.50 would be sent directly to my parents each month. Following Army orders, I also filed my will and applied for a $10,000 life insurance policy. This reinforced the hazardous nature of what I might expect as part of the Airborne forces.

---

[92] Bradley and Wood, Paratrooper, no pagination.
[93] [Pat] Davis, American Light Infantry Battles: Paratroopers, 1942-1945 (Reseda, CA, c. 1997), p. 331.

Chapter 3:
From Camp Mackall to the ETO

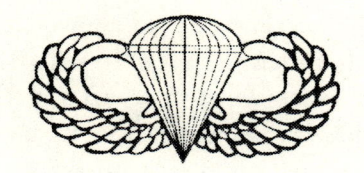

I know that you are concerned with the danger to be encountered by the airborne troops, but personally I do not think that we will be in any more danger of failing to return when this war is over than any other infantry troops. In fact, airborne troops are good and they know it, and I feel that the danger when they get into action will be on the other side.

General William M. Miley, Paratrooper

Pfc. Wilson (left) at Camp Mackall, 1943

464th PFAB Insignia

Colonel Edward S. Branigan, Jr.

I left Georgia for North Carolina, arriving at Camp Mackall in September 1943. This camp, the wartime post that served as the Headquarters of the Airborne Command, was located in Hoffman near Rockingham, North Carolina. There I was inducted into the 464th PFAB (Parachute Field Artillery Battalion). This battalion had only been activated on August 1, and it consisted of a Headquarters and Service Battery, three Firing Batteries, and an Anti-aircraft and Anti-tank Battery. All of its personnel were drawn from Ft. Benning's Parachute School and were placed under the command of Lt. Colonel Edward S. Branigan. Formerly a member of the National Guard, Branigan had graduated from the Command and General Staff School at Ft. Leavenworth in April 1942. He had served as Plans and Training officer of the 71st Field Artillery Brigade at Ft. Ethan Allen in Essex Junction, Vermont, and as Regimental Executive Officer of the 258th Field Artillery in Pine Camp, New York, before being called to Camp Mackall.

As a brief background, the "first airborne division headquartered at Camp Mackall was the 11th Airborne Division reporting on February 25, 1943. The 17th Airborne Division was activated there on April 25, 1943. The 13th Airborne Division was activated on August 13, 1943, and moved from Fort Bragg some forty miles to Camp Mackall in January 1944." The Camp, previously known as Camp Hoffman, was re-named in honor of Private John Thomas (Tommy) Mackall, from Wellsville, Ohio, who served in the 2nd Battalion, 503rd Parachute Infantry Regiment. "During the Allied invasion of North Africa in the airborne segment called Operation Torch, he was mortally wounded in an attack by French Vichy aircraft on his aircraft as it landed near Oran. Seven paratroopers died at the scene and several were wounded, including Mackall. He was evacuated by air to a British hospital at Gibraltar where he died on November 12, 1942."[94]

Compared to Ft. Benning, Camp Mackall seemed pretty sophisticated to me. It was composed of 1,750 buildings including heated barracks, a 1,200 bed hospital, 5 theaters, 6 beer gardens, and an all-weather airfield with three 5,000-foot runways. However, what stands out most in the mind of this farm boy from the Kansas Plains were the ever present sand and sand dunes covering the grounds and lots of tall pine trees. And to think, some "61,971 square acres of wilderness" had already been cleared out to make way for the Camp at the time of its construction.[95]

---

[94] "Camp Mackall: Home of the 'Airborne' in World War II." XVIII Airborne Corps & Fort Bragg. 6 April 2004 <http://www.bragg.army.mil/18abn/CampMackall.htm>.

[95] Devlin, Paratrooper, p. 193.

464th Cooks Robert Wilson (left) and Paul Thurman (right)

As we were deployed to Camp Mackall, I was assigned to Headquarters and Service Battery, and I happily chose to join as a cook. While growing up, I had learned to cook as needed on the farm, thus the work was hardly foreign to me. Three cooks in their "whites" and 3 KPs (Kitchen Police) in their fatigues worked each shift in the enlisted men's mess. The officers had their own mess hall and their own cooking staff. Our shift of cooks in the enlisted men's mess consisted of Sergeant Edward W. La Coste, Corporal Robert E. Truelove, and myself, a Private First Class. Cooks on the alternate shift included Sergeant Eddie Schmidt and John I. Dorsey, Jr, and we were regularly assisted by two other cooks by the surnames Weeks and Benoight.

Cook Wilson Peeling Potatoes

Our duties started right after the noon meal was served. We worked 24-hour on/off shifts. The beginning of each shift was literally a real mess. After the noon meal, the Mess Sergeant checked to see that all of the cooking staff was present, then we started in our preparations for the evening meal. After serving that meal, it was clean up time, after which we started planning for the next day's breakfast. We were usually done by 10:00 pm, after which we headed back to the barracks, showered, and hit the sack. 3:00 am would come around very soon. The Mess Sergeant woke us up, then we filed into the Mess Hall to prepare breakfast. After breakfast, the noon meal was prepared and served. Finally, we now had our time off.

Cook Wilson after the Meal

The cooks were exempt from several duties, including guard duty, KP duty, and parade duty, but we did have to keep up with rifle practice, required parachute jumps, physical exercise and some field excursions. The cooks knew more or less what they had to do with whatever they were given, and they were generally left alone to their work. Only once did I pull guard duty, and that was as an MP in the nearby town of Southern Pines.

In practical field exercises, we trained in squadrons, platoons, companies, and as a battalion. When possible, we combined our field excursions with other required duties. For example, if we needed to take food out to a unit that was involved in rifle practice, we usually got to do our rifle practice while we were out there serving meals to the rest of the troops. These particular assignments provided us good experience more like the situations we were likely to encounter when shipped overseas.

Cook Wilson with Mobile Kitchen in the Field

A high level of morale was maintained throughout the camp. This positive mental attitude shined through General Miley's 1943 Christmas message, delivered on December 24: "Tomorrow is Christmas and it is my great regret that due to the strenuous training program that all of you cannot be with your families on that day. I wish to take this opportunity to express to each and every officer and man of this Division my sincere thanks for the splendid cooperation and fine spirit with which you have worked since joining this Division. A continuation of the spirits and hard work you have displayed in the past is bound to pay dividends in enabling us to succeed in battle without severe losses. I feel sure that if the rest of the Army can rise to the high level set by you, that we will be able to celebrate July 4th in Tokyo and next Christmas at home."[96]

Periodically, we made required parachute jumps. Some of these were performed at Camp Mackall whereas at other times we jumped at Ft. Bragg, some forty miles away. Some sources suggest that troopers

---

[96] Daily Bulletin, No. 250, 24 December 1943. Headquarters 17th Airborne Division, Camp Mackall. William M. Miley Papers, Box 1, "17th Airborne Division Daily Bulletins" Folder, USAMHI.

were required to make a jump a month to keep their wings, but once again, perhaps the cooks did not average quite as many jumps as those pursuing other detail duties. I made a jump every two to three months, totaling 6 between September 1943 and February 1945. On one of these jumps, we were outfitted in full gear to allow us to feel the effect of the weight which we would be expected to carry into combat.

Wade C. Hinson, 464th PFAB

Whereas some paratroopers performed night jumps while stationed at Mackall during this time, I was never called upon to do so. Wade C. Hinson, one of the 464th, recalls that night jumps added considerable hazards. During "the first night jump I made at Camp Mackall," Hinson claimed, "the pilot thought we were near the drop zone and turned the red light on to signal us to stand up, hook up, and get ready to exit the plane. After the pilot decided [that] we were nowhere near the drop zone . . ., [he] instructed the Jumpmaster [to] have us sit back down. When the Jumpmaster yelled "Sit Down" to the troopers, the [first] trooper in the lead stick exited the plane." Later, "we were told a search team was sent to look for him with no success. He arrived back in Camp about two weeks later."[97] Another nighttime jump incident occurred in a different battalion stationed at Mackall. In this incident, "several men" unintentionally ended up in a lake.[98]

We were continually challenged physically at Camp Mackall, and always mindful to "Keep Alert." Parachuting itself, however, was a little less complicated here, primarily because all of the chute packing was left to the "riggers," those paratroopers of top-notch ability who were specifically designated to parachute cleaning and packing duties.

We relied wholeheartedly upon the riggers; indeed, they held our lives in their hands. They were always there with quips like, "Hey, if it doesn't open, bring it back. I'll repack it!," and "It's Good to the Last Drop!" Still, in reality, they took their obligations most seriously, as is attested by their pledge:

I will keep constantly in mind that until men grow wings their parachutes must be dependable.

I will pack every parachute as though I am to jump with it myself, and will stand ready to jump with any parachute which I have certified as properly inspected and repacked.

I will remember always that the other man's life is as dear to him as mine is to me.

I will never resort to guesswork, as I know that chance is a fool's god, and that I, a rigger, cannot depend on it.

I will never pass over any defect nor neglect any repair, no matter how small, as I know that omissions and mistakes in the rigging of a parachute may cost a life.

I will keep all parachute equipment entrusted to my care in the best possible condition, remembering always that little things left undone cause major troubles.

---

[97] Wade C. Hinson to Robert L. Wilson, December 13, 2003.
[98] Wade C. Hinson to Robert L. Wilson, December 13, 2003.

> I will never sign my name to a parachute inspection or packing certificate unless I have personally performed or directly supervised every step and am entirely satisfied with all the work.
>
> I will never let the idea that a piece of work is "good enough" make me a potential murderer through a careless mistake or oversight, for I know there can be no compromise with perfection.
>
> I will keep always a wholehearted respect for my vocation, regarding it as a high profession rather than a day-to-day task, and will keep ever in mind my grave responsibility.
>
> I will be sure – always.[99]

Our initial training at Ft. Benning had been focused on making our jumps. The attitude at Camp Mackall reinforced that "the actual jumping is the least important part" of our training. Here, we were further developed as a "specialist fighter" who used a parachute "merely to get to the place where . . . [we were to be] of most use."[100] Brigadier General Ridgely Gaither, Commandant of Airborne Command, claimed the parachute is but the "most modern form of the oldest and most dependable fighting unit, the foot-soldier." The "aspiring parachutist," Gaither continued, "has to remember that his work only begins when he" hits the ground. His "duty" is to "get there with plenty of enemy hurting equipment." The paratrooper must know how to "land primed in A-1 physical shape to do his work on the ground." An "ambulance full" of paratroopers who jump incorrectly "presents very little worry to an opponent."[101]

We had not pursued any artillery practice while at Ft. Benning, but resumed that part of our training at Camp Mackall. In addition to our artillery practice there, on March 20, 1944, we departed North Carolina for Camp Blanding, in Jacksonville, Florida, where we were stationed through July 26. Camp Blanding was the site of a large

---

[99] Bradley and Wood, <u>Paratrooper</u>, no pagination.
[100] Ayling, <u>They Fly to Fight</u>, p. 41.
[101] Ayling, <u>They Fly to Fight</u>, p. 45.

Infantry Replacement Training Center (IRTC) under the command of Brigadier General E. W. Fales. One of every three weeks in Florida was devoted to overhead artillery demonstrations. We had trucked our artillery down to Florida, and we fired our artillery over Blanding's infantry to simulate the combat conditions that their infantry were likely to encounter. This opportunity also allowed us to set up and maneuver our weapons over a terrain that was unfamiliar to us.

Our time in Florida provided ample opportunity for boasting of the physical prowess of paratroopers. We staged several "double-timing" demonstrations for local staff officers, and we carried out a "10-game, Center-wide softball tournament" during which the troopers suffered only two defeats.[102] On a personal note, this stint at Camp Blanding also allowed me several short visits with my brother, John, who was stationed there in the infantry before he was shipped off to Austria.

---

[102] "464th Battalion leaves IRTC after serving here four months," Unidentified newspaper clipping, authors' collection.

John Wilson, U.S. Army, WWII

While at Camp Blanding, twenty-four troopers from our battalion performed a mass jump during the IRTC's observation of "Infantry Day" on Thursday, June 15 – nine days after our "brothers" in the 82nd and 101st Divisions had jumped at the "D-Day" invasion of Normandy, France. The Camp Blanding jump took place between 4:30 and 5:00 pm., immediately before Major General Harry W. Hazlett's "Infantry Day" address.

Paratroopers, viewed as "the darlings of the Army," were "often called upon to jump in demonstrations" as well as to "participate in maneuvers."[103] While in Florida, we all were involved in an exhibition War Bond jump at the Duvall County Fairgrounds. As recorded shortly after this jump, 288 members of the 464th PFAB arrived in twelve C-47 transport planes, escorted by a "squadron of Navy pursuit planes," creating such a force that "the ground began to shake." Over Stewart Field the planes "roared in echelons of three and out of the lead plane came 'Oscar,' the traditional parachute dummy who indicated wind direction." After another pass over the field, "held up for a few minutes by a train passing nearby," the planes came in at 600 feet to discharge "in perfect order" 96 men, eight in a stick, from each of twelve planes. A "bedlam of screams" was heard as the first man "hit the silk," but was "suddenly hushed as the white chutes billowed out and the first waves landed down field." They had "float[ed] to earth" this Thursday evening in "the largest public demonstration ever staged by Army parachutists in this part of Florida."[104]

As the second (of three) waves of planes soared overhead, the announcer James F. Murphy, asked his listeners, "What would you do if those were enemy planes?" To which the "thrilled crowd yelled back, 'Buy bonds'." The mass jump was the "highlight" of Jacksonville's huge Fifth War Bond rally, and "it attracted thousands of persons to the Duval County Fairground – [the] landing field for the paratroopers." One reporter estimated that some 35,000 people "jammed inside the grounds," while another 25,000 "witnessed the spectacle from homes and cars parked as far as 10 blocks in all directions." An estimated $17,000 of bonds were purchased that day.[105]

---

[103] Davis, <u>American Light Infantry Battles</u>, p. 332.

[104] "Thousands Greet Sky Troopers and Buy Bonds," Unidentified newspaper clipping, authors' collection.

[105] "Thousands Greet Sky Troopers and Buy Bonds," Unidentified newspaper clipping, authors' collection.

The equipment used in airborne warfare was "displayed prominently on the fairground." Featured in the exhibit was this branch's principal weapon – the 75 mm pack howitzer. Formerly a "Mountain gun," the high speed 75 mm was an ideal airborne artillery and anti-tank gun. It was ideal in that it was the heaviest weapon available for trooper drops from planes or gliders. Also on view for the public were "50 caliber machine guns, with ground and anti-aircraft mounts, and the famed Bazooka." After their initial jump, the paratroopers then proceeded to nearby Hemming Park "in time to participate in a war bond rally scheduled there at 6:30 o'clock."[106]

Some of the exhibition jumps made during this era were used, in part, as paratrooper recruitment. That was not the case when I first heard of the parachute troops at Camp Beale in California. I never saw a parachute jump before I got to Georgia.

Pfc. Wilson on Break outside Barracks

We returned to Camp Mackall on July 27, 1944 where we remained until early 1945. Camp life there was much like that recorded in many other WW II accounts.[107] We spent a considerable amount of time standing around. Hurry, hurry, hurry – wait, wait, wait. Army life has

---

[106] Leroy Thompson, <u>U.S. Airborne in Action</u>. Combat Troops Number 10. (Carrollton, TX: Squadron/Signal Publications, Inc., 1992), p. 12.

[107] For a general overview of soldier life at base, in camps, and at the front, see Lee Kennett, <u>GI: The American Soldier in World War II</u> (New York: Charles Scribner's Sons, 1987).

long been one of waiting for that next order, and then following it through to its completion. Radios in our barracks as well as the <u>Stars and Stripes</u> newspaper kept us well informed of the recent actions in both of the theaters of war. I played a fair amount of softball and, twice a month or so, wrote letters home.

As others have remarked, U.S. soldiers rarely turned down an opportunity to get drunk. Historian William O'Neill claimed that "America floated to victory [in World War II] in a tidal wave of booze."[108] I guess that I was part of that tidal wave when off duty. Yet, as we were continually reminded, drinking binges had their potential downsides. Drunken sexual exploits could easily lead to VD which would, in turn, diminish the strength of our country's fighting force. To further instill this message, we were treated to monthly sexual hygiene lectures and routinely subjected to fallout in "Raincoats and overshoes" for our "short arm" (i.e., VD) medical inspections.

In November 1944, we were encouraged to vote. The presidential candidates running for election were the incumbent, Franklin Roosevelt and his challenger, Wendell Wilkie. Reporters alerted soldiers in various formats. We read of this in <u>The Talon</u>, the newspaper of the 17th Airborne Division. <u>Talon</u> reporters remarked, "Congress spent three months, thousands of dollars, and millions of words to make it possible for you to vote. Don't waste all of that time, money, and effort." We were alerted that "in ample time prior to the November election" we would "get a ballot from the Secretary of [our] home state." We could then mark our choice of candidates and "send it right back to the Secretary, airmail free."[109] Voting seemed as much of a duty as did fighting for our country – a task for which we were being prepared.

On February 4, 1945, we departed Mackall and arrived the following day at the New York Port of Embarkation at Camp Shanks, some thirty miles north of New York City on the Hudson River. We were not allowed to wear any insignia (i.e., wings or shoulder patches), or even boots, that would identify us as paratroopers. As WW II historian Stephen E. Ambrose pointed out, "enemy spies might see

---

[108] William O'Neil, <u>A Democracy at War</u>, as cited by Kirk B. Ross, <u>The Skymen: A Parachute Rifle Company's Story of the Battle of the Bulge and the Jump Across the Rhine</u> (Atglen, PA: Schiffer Military History, 2000), p. 90.

[109] Davis, <u>American Light Infantry Battles</u>, p. 333.

them and would know that an airborne division was shipping out."[110] While at Camp Shanks, I received a good round of inoculations. Some men were troubled by their physical reactions to these shots, but I had no complaints. No one was given leave at this point, but it took quite some time to get 5000 soldiers officially prepared for their overseas crossing. Within a week, I was aboard the U.S.S. General William Weigel (AP-119) with 5000 other rotation troops as it left New York on February 11.[111]

USS Gen. William Weigel (AP-119)

William Weigel (1863-1936) graduated from the U.S. Military Academy at West Point in 1887. After fighting as an officer in the Indian Wars, he participated in the Cuban campaign during the Spanish-American War and was active in the Philippine Insurrection. As a division commander during World War I, he led troops in the

---

[110] Stephen E. Ambrose, <u>Band of Brothers: E Company, 506th Regiment, 101st Airborne from Normandy to Hitler's Eagle's Nest</u> (New York: Simon & Schuster, 2001 Classic Edition), p. 41.

[111] Paraphrased from "USS General William Weigel, AP-119." <u>U.S. Coast Guard</u>. August 2001 <http://www.uscg.mil/hq/g-cp/history/WEBCUTTERS/G_Weigel.html>.

Aisne-Marne offensive and the Meuse-Argonne campaign. Following that war he served as Chief of Staff, Department of the East. Weigel later served as a divisional commander and, in 1927, headed the Philippine Department.

Originally named General C.H. Barth, the ship we traveled on was renamed General William Weigel on August 24, 1944, and was acquired by the U.S. Navy in January 1945. Our trip was her maiden voyage in service to the armed forces. As we sailed off, we watched the Statue of Liberty "disappear" in the distance. Many soldiers wondered if they would ever see this U.S. monument of freedom again. We were part of an extremely long convoy of ships, surrounded by other battleships and tankers. Indeed, all I could see were miles of ships both fore and aft.

Before we had left the New York harbor, the ship's tilting to and fro caused many aboard to get sea sick. Seeing this, and receiving the advice of others, encouraged me to take an upper bunk (actually a hammock) in our lower deck quarters. Of course, many troopers continued to have troubles overcoming airsickness on planes, too. After all, we were not recruited to ride in planes but to jump out, and nearly all of us had never been in a plane before our first jump. At times, I really thought that it was unreal to be riding something that, to me, was so novel as this huge ship. We do not see many of these vessels in landlocked Kansas. Life aboard ship was, at times, even comical. For example, at mess time, we stood up eating from our metal trays while holding them down on the narrow metal stalls on which we had placed them. As the ship tilted, long rows of soldiers grabbed their trays, at least for the first few meals. Some, unfortunately, were not quick enough.

The weather was cold, but not icy, and the waters were rough from time to time. We were thankful for the woolen sweaters and wristlets that we had been given right before we left North Carolina to help combat any cold weather we encountered en route to or while we served in the European Theater of Operations (ETO). During days aboard the Weigel, we performed calisthenics on the deck and dressed in our fatigues or pretty much as we wanted since no dress code was in effect. We were, however, required to wear life jackets any time we walked on the ship's decks. This extra bit of bulk made us feel even more like tightly packed sardines in a can. All GIs showered with salt water except for those with special medical needs. Overall, we did not do much of anything – except win or lose at cards or dice – all during this transport trip.

Thinking back, I clearly recall that throughout this Atlantic voyage, I never saw so many people get so damned sick. We felt sorry for those who could simply not hold anything in their stomachs. Perhaps it does take a different breed of an individual, or at least different training, to get used to Navy life. Even though I did not get into the Navy when I was drafted in 1942, at least now I had a little sense of life at sea.

After thirteen days at sea, we landed at Le Havre, France, and disembarked the U.S.S. General William Weigel on February 24 – my twenty second birthday. As we were coming into port and while walking down the long pier, I recall seeing a number of sunken boats around the harbor. These were the first actual signs of war that we had seen anywhere other than in moving pictures.

Harbor, Le Havre, France

It was good to be off the water and on solid ground once again. We, the 464th PFAB, were trucked off to Camp Lucky Strike on the same day. It felt good to be approaching combat. It was time to fight. Let's do it. Let's get this war over with.

Camp Lucky Strike was situated near the towns of Janville and Saint-Sylvian, France, some 3 miles from Saint-Valery-en Caux. Identifying these camps with names like "Chesterfield," "Philip Morris," "Old Gold," "Twenty Grand," "Pall Mall," and "Lucky Strike" attests to the popularity of smoking amongst the soldiers.

Our camp was one of several "tent cities" where replacement soldiers in transit were temporarily stationed. Many battalions were stationed there with us, some 100,000 men filling the camp each day. Camp Luck Strike extended over 600 hectares where, over the course of the war, some 1,500,000 U.S. soldiers spent at least a couple days. Here in this tent city, one could find, "like in any American city, a hospital, church, movie theater, post office, police station, barber shop, and a supermarket. There were also concerts and shows with famous celebrities. And around the camp, there were the usual prostitutes and easy access to the local black market."[112]

---

[112] Al D'Ambra. "The Cigarette Camps: The U.S. Army Camps in the Le Havre Area." September 2002. 225th AAA Searchlight Battalion Veterans Association. 24 May 2004 <http://www.skylighters.org/special/cigcamps/cmplstrk.html>.

These "tent cities" or "cigarette camps" also had public parks, and "in certain places, statues of pretty women." The Red Cross had offices set up where nurses and girls served hot coffee, cake, and newspapers day and night. Elsewhere in the camp one found the bars: one for officers, another for NCOs and soldiers. "One could drink everything they used to in pre-war France: the best liqueurs, good champagne, cognacs, and water of life (aqua vita), as well as Coca-Cola, whiskey, gin, and American beer. The bars were only open from 7:00 to 10:00 p.m., which was not enough time to satisfy the customers."

The camp also contained "a PX and several gift shops." The PX "carried everything — one could find handkerchiefs, electric razors, chocolates, condoms, cigarettes, cigars, toothbrushes, lighters, watches, and knives." In the gift shops GIs could purchase Parisian perfume, scarves, lace, and jewelry to send to their mothers, wives, and girlfriends back home. Each section of the camp also contained "a hospital, shot clinic, and . . . VD clinics. Condoms were available everywhere and the soldiers really needed them, since the camp was assaulted, day and night, by an army of women!"[113]

Upon arrival at Lucky Strike, we were given the winged golden unicorn insignia of the 13th Airborne Division. Tradition associated the unicorn with the qualities of virtue, courage, and strength – all necessities of the paratrooper. The 13th Airborne (the "Golden Unicorns") were activated on August 13 (Friday the 13th), 1943 at Ft. Bragg, North Carolina, under the command of Major General George W. Griner, Jr., and had received deployment orders in January 1945. They left for France on January 26, now under the command of Major General Eldridge G. Chapman, and were assigned to the XVIIIth Airborne Corps upon their arrival into the ETO. By the time of my arrival, in late February, 1945, the XVIII Corps consisted of the 82nd, 101st, 17th and now the 13th Airborne Divisions, all under the Corps Command of the previous 82nd Division Commander, Major General Matthew B. Ridgway. Ridgway had succeeded Major General Omar N. Bradley as commander of the 82nd Airborne Division on June 26, 1942, after having served as Bradley's assistant. The 13th Airborne settled into

---

[113] Al D'Ambra. "The Cigarette Camps."

assembly areas around the French cities of Seans, Joigny and Auxerre, some seventy-five miles southeast of Paris.

13th Airborne Division Insignia

After arriving in the ETO, the 13th Airborne Division was reorganized into two parachute and one glider divisions. The composition of the

Division at that time, before the 464th PFAB was attached, included the following units: 326th Glider Infantry Regiment, 515th and 517th Parachute Infantry Regiments, 458th and 460th Parachute Field Artillery Battalions, 676th and 677th Glider Field Artillery Battalions, 409th Airborne Quartermaster Company, 513th Airborne Signal Company, 129th Airborne Engineer Battalion, 153rd Airborne Anti-Aircraft Battalion, 222nd Airborne Medical Company, 13th Parachute Maintenance Company, Headquarters Special Troops, Headquarters Company, Military Police Platoon, and the 713th Airborne Ordnance Maintenance Company.[114]

Soon after our arrival, we set up our cooking kitchen when it arrived to the camp by truck. We also set up our sleeping tents, four men to a tent, close to the kitchen. Sgt. La Coste, Cpl. Truelove, and I remained one shift of cooks just as we had been in the States. Our tent mates were all kitchen workers. That arrangement helped, in part, due to the fact that the morning shift cooks had to rise early (between 0300 and 0400 hours) to get started preparing the meal.

As in the States, the cooks were exempt from having to pull guard duty and other drills. Still, everyone was expected to keep fit through calisthenics, and we kept checking and cleaning our personal and battalion equipment over and over again. Our howitzers had been dipped in cosmoline, a combination of grease, shellac and beeswax with copper sulfate added as a corrosion inhibitor, before departing New York in order to protect them from the salty ocean air and water. Removing this paraffin-like grease from the exterior and bores of the cannons in France required laborious effort with kerosene and putty knives. We knew that we were training for big combat duty somewhere, we just did not know when or where we would be called. Time was of the essence, though, and we were alerted to always be prepared. Still, all we could do was to wait.

The weather was cold in France that February. Frost frequently covered the ground, but we were not bothered by the freezing conditions anywhere near what our fellow combat men had recently been exposed

---

[114] George Larson, "13th Airborne Division: 'Thrice Called, Thrice Denied,'" The Airborne Quarterly 15 (2002): 48. For a history of the 13th Airborne Division, see "13th Airborne Division, Training History" c. 1946, USAMHI.

to in Bastogne, Belgium. Still, we had to keep well clothed against the cold weather. The four-burner gas cooking stoves that we used in the kitchen kept us warm while we worked. Each sleeping tent was also equipped with a wood burning stove whose flue rose up through an opening on the tent's roof. Upon arrival, we were rationed a little bit of wood as we set up camp. However, after that initial supply had been used up, we were on our own to gather the wood we needed to heat our own tent.

One day, while scavenging for wood, several of us noticed a railroad line that was laid nearby. Upon closer inspection, we found several loose railroad ties. It was not too difficult to pull one of these out. What a great source of wood! We extracted one tie, skipped a few, leaving plenty of space on the line with ties intact, and then pulled another. We carried these back to our tent and chopped them up using the hatchet axes and knives that were supplied. Those ties gave us plenty of wood and we knew that they would keep us warm for quite some time. However, after a few days, we were instructed not to take any more ties. How our superiors found out about our "resourcefulness" I never learned. The rail line still worked well. I know this from having ridden a train car – a "40 & 8" (forty men or eight horses) – over these lines to and from local villages on a few occasions. Still, I suppose that our adventure adds to what others have claimed, "it was staggering how fast," particularly on foreign soil, that some men "could get into trouble."[115]

As a further measure to keep warm at night in our tents, when we could find paper, we put it beneath our sleeping bags in order to help block the coldness that had settled on the hard ground. Working as a cook, I had a ready supply of the paper sacks that had once contained 100 pounds of sugar. We also had those itchy wool blankets for heaping on top of us to help get us through the cold nights. When working around the camp, nearly everyone wore some type of headgear – a woolen cap or a pith helmet – to keep our heads warm.

We each had one duffle bag in which we kept all of our personal belongings and clothing. Although we had our Class A uniforms including our short Eisenhower jackets with us, we only wore them

---

[115] Ross, <u>The Skymen</u>, p. 263.

if we wanted to dress up when we went to the village. Otherwise we wore our fatigues around camp, with our long johns beneath, and an overcoat when needed. We wore combat boots around the camp, saving our paratrooper boots for anytime we needed to dress in Class A attire.

While in France, we cooks had to learn to work with new kinds of supplies. Milk, potatoes, and eggs were supplied only in dehydrated form. The menu assignments had come in through Headquarters, and we stuck to them as well as our supplies allowed. Whenever possible, I scoured about the region's farmhouses for fresh eggs, but relatively few were found. Spam, however, was available in abundance. Back at Mackall, cold cuts with Spam was the traditional Sunday evening meal. Here, it became one of our staples. Bugs and rodents were not too much of a problem in our cooking kitchen. We did lay out mouse traps and powders for precaution, but I do not recall having to clean the traps of too many rodents.

Soon we learned the ease of obtaining French bread from nearby villages, and we routinely sent men into the villages where the French were willing to trade their bread for nearly anything. Not knowing anything of the French language, we cooks soon found out that small amounts of coffee, chocolate, and cigarettes were particularly useful in securing our supplies of bread – and almost anything else we wanted.[116] Ross Carter recalled that "many girls could fall in love for a chocolate bar or a few cigarettes."[117]

French wines and liquor were also readily available when we went into surrounding villages. Thinking back, I recall how strange it seemed to me that the French lived in 'apartments' above their livestock that were gathered on the ground floor at street level. Most of the village inhabitants seem to have been older people. I'm not sure where the kids of the villages were at this time.

Although this area had once been occupied by the Germans and had been heavily bombed by the British, engineers of the American

---

[116] Back in Camp Mackall, a soldier named Bright worked as our baker, but Bright was not among the 464th that crossed the Atlantic.

[117] R. S. Carter, Those Devils in Baggy Pants, p. 3.

forces reworked the area beginning the month following the August 25, 1944 liberation of Paris, and the living conditions seemed to be in good order. By the time I arrived in the camp, many of the bomb craters had been filled in order to make the terrain more useable.

On March 1, a new Table of Operation (TOE) was established, and we of the 464th were reassigned, this time to the 17th Airborne Division. March has always been a transition month in Europe in terms of weather. Many of us hoped that the winds of war would be quieted for good during this particular March.

The 13th Division was ultimately scratched from the upcoming mission. The story that I have always recalled is that there were not enough planes available to support the air transport required for both the 13th and the 17th Divisions. Following the massive loss of planes and gliders over the previous nine months, it appears to be true that there were only enough air resources to drop two divisions. However, as the Brits were to hold supreme command over the upcoming operation, they demanded that one of their Airborne divisions be used. So, "acceding to their request because of the need to retain good relations," the 13th Airborne was scratched.[118] Many that I knew in the 13th Division were downhearted about getting pulled from this mission – the third time they were pulled so close to active combat. Only a few that I knew of in the 13th viewed this action as a "life saver."

The 17th Airborne, the Golden Eagle Claw Division, had been activated on April 15, 1943 at Camp Mackall, the second Division "born" at this Camp. They were deployed to Europe a year later, arriving in Ogbourne St. George, England on August 26, 1944. There, under the Corps Command of Major General Matthew Ridgway, the 17th Airborne continued their preparation and training on bases in England. Upon hearing of the German entrapment of the 101st Airborne in Bastogne, the 17th Airborne was hastily flown to the continent and was employed as ground troops to cut off the German penetration. Members of the 17th entered combat on Christmas Day, "pitted against several [German] Panzer Armies," and fought in this Battle of the Bulge for 65 days under the "abominable conditions of snow, ice and

---

[118] G. Larson, "13th Airborne Division," p. 48.

93

fog, [and] freezing winds," with "poor [military] intelligence, no air cover and insufficient artillery support against tanks."[119] Their tenacity and forcefulness led to the German withdrawal of forces, and the 17th Airborne took the towns of Espeller, Wiltz, and Eschweiler. Moreover, the action in Bastogne had ennobled the U.S. Airborne in the minds of the Germans as "immortal madmen" who "charged through the heaviest barrage of shell fire with utter disregard for its stinging blast."[120] Then, on February 10, 1945, with the Germans in retreat, the 17th Airborne was withdrawn to Chalons-sur-Marne – the site of Attila's defeat in 451 A.D. – near Rheims, for "re-equipping training" and preparation for an airborne assault across the Rhine River.[121]

Upon their arrival in the vicinity of the camp, it was apparent that much "housekeeping" was in order. As General Miley later recounted, "the spring thaws had made the ground a sea of mud" and the roads were "practically impassable."[122] Four days were allocated for settlement into this area, then the attention was turned toward troop training and preparing for the airborne operation.

More groundwork was required in other areas of allied airborne encampment. Considerable effort was expended to "improve run-ways and to build taxi-tracks, marshalling areas, dispersal areas and access roads, to fill bomb craters, repair drainage and lay glider parks and to improve accommodation for stores, officers and men." Under IX Troop Carrier Commander Colonel Branse Burbridge, some three thousand U.S., British, and Canadian army engineers and 750 French civilians worked shifts over a month-long 24 hour/day schedule to prepare the grounds.[123]

On March 11, members of the 464th PFAB departed Camp Lucky Strike and were transferred to join the 17th Airborne at Chalons-sur-Marne. To mark that juncture, we were given the Eagle's Golden Talon

---

[119] William Tom, "17th Airborne Division@miltary.com. August 16 2000. Military. com Unit Pages. 5 February 2004 http://www.miltary.com/HomePage/UnitPageH istory/1,13506,700490/702423,00.html>.

[120] Donald R. Pay, Thunder From Heaven: Story of the 17th Airborne Division 1943-1945 (Nashville, TN: Battery Press, 1980 reprint), p. 22.

[121] Hagerman, "General Miley and 'His' Division," p. 21.

[122] "Historical Report of Operation Varsity," 17th Airborne Division, 1945, forward.

[123] Napier Crookenden, Airborne at War (Shepperton, Surrey: Ian Allan, 1978), p. 85.

as our Division's shoulder patch. This insignia symbolized a "surprise strike from the darkness of the sky" and the "grasping of golden opportunities in battle below."[124]

17th Airborne Division Insignia

At the time, the 17th Division was composed of the following units: Headquarters and Headquarters Company, Special Troops, Multinational Military Police Platoon, a Division Band, Reconnaissance Platoon, 717th Ordnance Maintenance Company, 411th Quartermasters Company, 517th Signal Company, a Parachute Maintenance Company, 224th Medical Company, 139th Engineers Battalion, 155th Anti-Aircraft Battalion, Headquarters Battery (Artillery), 464th and 466th Parachute Field Artillery Battalions, 680th and 681st Glider Field Artillery Battalions, 507th and 513th Parachute Infantry, and the 196th Glider

---

124 B. Hageman, "17th Airborne Division," in B. Hagerman (ed) U.S.A. Airborne 50th Anniversary, 1940-1990 (Paducah, KY: Turner Publishing Co., 1990), p. 190, and D.R.Pay, Thunder from Heaven, p. 13.

Infantry. Attached units included the 1st Commando Brigade, 771st Tank Battalion, 605th Tank Destroyer Battalion, 692nd Field Artillery Battalion, 387th Anti-Aircraft Artillery Automatic Weapons Battalion, Company A, 3rd Chemical Battalion, and seven regiments of the 53rd Division Artillery group.

In the words of 464th commanding officer, Lt. Col. Branigan, the Division Artillery, commanded by Brigadier General J. W. Phelps "welcomed us, and was most helpful with information [and] assistance." During this planning stage for Operation Varsity, the 17th worked to "expedite the arrival and final equipping" of our battalion.[125] This assistance was especially appreciated, Branigan continued, "because the 464th was the only unit in the Division without combat experience." This reception was in striking contrast to the "always coolly distant" Division Headquarters and Staff who "never really made us feel accepted as an integral part of the Div[ision]." The unit that at Ft. Blanding, Florida, had become known as "Branigan's Braves" now became known as "Branigan's Bastards" – "It was [as if we were] the bastard son at the family reunion." We were never to be "organic to the 17th [Division]."

Colonel Edson D. Raff

At Chalons, the 464th was assigned by the Division to the 507th Combat Team that was at that time being formed under the command

[125] "Historical Report of Operation Varsity," p. 12.

of Colonel Edson D. Raff, the commander of the 507th Parachute Infantry Regiment ("Raff's Ruffians"). Raff, known as "Little Caesar" to his men, was of the "stocky, diminutive" stature that was seen as "ideal size and weight" for a paratrooper.[126] Raff had amused the British and U.S. upper brass at a March 8 briefing in General Miley's Headquarters in Rheims. Like other regimental commanders, Raff was asked to explain how he would carry out his mission. While indicating precise positions on a wall map, he explained, "The 507th are flying in west to east and jumping here. We get together here. In these woods are a bunch of Heines and we sort 'em out." As he concluded, he received a "ripple of admiring laughter."[127]

The 507th Combat Team comprised 2476 soldiers, 2100 infantrymen and 379 artillerymen.[128] Branigan was designated as the commander of "Group Branigan," his own 464th together with the 680th Glider Field Artillery Battalion. Col. Raff held "complete confidence" in Branigan, and their work together was "most harmonious."

We all respected Lt. Col. Branigan. He was a "Good Joe," and he was very good to us. He would back up his men 100%. Although we men of the 464th had long been banded together through our special service training, we now truly felt as if we were banded together like brothers. That "Band of Brothers" imagery so often and rightly used in discussion of the 101st Airborne Division was a belief commonly held by each of the battalions within all of the airborne divisions of WW II.

Life in this camp was pretty much as it had been at Lucky Strike. I kept up my duties as before. We did, however, receive much more information about the kind of combat that was occurring and the types of action that we might see. Although the valiant efforts of the 17th Division in Bastogne were well known to us by this time through radio news and reporting in the Stars & Stripes and The Yank, we did not intermingle with those from other units. As in instances throughout this and other wars, many seasoned combat veterans kept their distance from those young, green replacements that they considered to be "all

---

[126] Gregory, United States Airborne Forces, p. 39.

[127] Crookenden, Airborne at War, p. 92.

[128] Clay Blair, Ridgway's Paratroopers: The American Airborne in World War II (New York: Dial Press, 1985), p. 453.

piss and vinegar." As a replacement, I had no real idea of what combat was going to be like. The only concept I had was from what I had seen in training films. But the movies could not begin to convey the feeling of really being there under fire. Still, the "seasoned" members of the 507th knew that we were all there for the same reason and in but a short time, they showed us considerable respect.

On March 15, it had become evident that the 464th was "fully equipped and ready for combat," and the Division's artillery plan for the assault was finalized.[129] After ten days in Chalons, the forward echelon of the 464th, of which I was a part, departed and was sequestered into the Marshalling Area adjacent to Airfield A-80.[130] It seemed, at the time, that the entire 17th Division was gathered there within the woven-wire fenced area. Now we knew that a new kind of action was approaching.

---

[129] "Historical Report of Operation Varsity," p. 16.

[130] The Rear echelon of the Battalion was sent to Sonnis, Belgium. [Edward S. Branigan], "History of Services, 464th Parachute Field Artillery Battalion," no date, p. 3, "Rhine River Crossing. 17th ABN Div." Folder, William B. Breuer Papers, Box 3, World War II Units, 17th Airborne Division, USAMHI.

Chapter 4:
Red Light – March 1945 Preparations

Over the Rhine, then, let us go. And good hunting to you all on the other side.

Field Marshal Sir Bernard L. Montgomery

Once sequestered and sealed into the Marshalling Area we were grouped with some 1200 other troopers. We learned over the loud speakers on March 23 that on the next day we were going to jump over the Rhine River.[131] In a historic and symbolic sense, the Rhine had

---

[131] The capacity of each Marshalling Area was consistent, except for those who were to drop from C-46s, which were capped at 2600. "Historical Report of Operation Varsity," p. 12. General Brereton had decided to go ahead with the launch and notified Montgomery who sent a message to all commanders before 1700 on the 23rd stating that all operations "would be mounted as planned." "Narrative of Operation Varsity," p. 6.

long served as a tactical barrier. No enemy force had ventured across it since Napoleon's invasion in 1800.[132] The river alone, running 825 miles from Switzerland to the North Sea, presented a "natural moat" to western Germany that "forc[ed] any invader from the west to pause before attempting to cross it."[133]

We were also informed on March 23 that there would be other planes coming in to join ours as part of a massive jump – though it was difficult to visualize at the time the actual scale of the jump that was planned. This jump would take place in daylight so that the troops would have improved odds of landing more precisely and completely in their designated DZs than some troops had on previous airborne invasions during the war.

As fair warning, we were told that casualties could be nearly 50%. We all shook hands with one another realizing that one of each pair of hand shakers might not be around tomorrow night. I'm sure that the men of the 17th who had already seen considerable combat braced up even more as the casualty predictions were laid out before us. Our official briefing was "to be so complete" that every enlisted man would know "the 'big picture,' the plan for the division, the plan for his unit, and what he as an individual was going to do on landing."[134]

A large "operations tent" had been set up as the Division's War Room. Nearby, we saw the "sand tables" on which the topographies of the regions surrounding our DZs were laid out. Tactical reconnaissance aircraft flyovers had secured aerial photos from which these realistic dioramas of hills, rivers, and roads had been constructed. Lt. Col. Branigan met with all of us in the 464th to let us know the specifics about plans for the following day.

---

[132] Dean M. Bressler, "Allied Forces Breach the Rhine," Assembly 53 (1995): 24.

[133] John Pimlott, "Crossing the Rhine," in Tony Hall (ed) March to Victory: The Final Months of WWII from D-Day, June 6, 1944 to the Fall of Japan, August 14, 1945 (New York: Crescent Books, 1944), p. 129. For a more complete geohistory of the Rhine, see Mark Cioc, The Rhine: An Eco-Biography, 1815-2000 (Seattle: University of Washington Press, 2002).

[134] "Historical Report of Operation Varsity," p. 17.

Discussing Rhine Jump over Sand Tables

We also knew that the attack was not going to be a complete surprise. The Germans knew when we were planning to jump the river, and they even knew that we would be coming in around Wesel. Allied signal intelligence was aware that Hitler and the German High Command (the *Oberkommando der Wehrmacht*) knew of an impending air attack over the Rhine. According to William B. Breuer's historical account, "A captured Wehrmacht document outlined defense measures to be taken against an assault from the sky. At secluded Bletchley Park, 40 miles north of London, supersecret Ultra intercepted a series of coded German radio messages warning that the Allied airborne onslaught would hit between Wesel and Duisburg."[135] Apparently, this was known by the Germans as early as 8 days prior to the attack (D-8).[136]

At the soldier's level, we learned of this over the loudspeakers set up in the mess halls. There, we listened to Axis Sally, that propaganda bitch on the German radio making statements like "Come on 17th we

---

[135] Operation Ultra was designed to intercept and decode German signals sent using Enigma, the top-secret German cypher machine. William B. Breuer, <u>Geronimo: American Paratroopers in World War II</u> (New York: St. Martins, 1989), p. 540. For a thorough overview of Enigma, see Hugh Sebag-Montefiore, <u>Enigma: The Battle for the Code</u> (New York: John Wiley, 2001).

[136] Pay, <u>Thunder From Heaven</u>, p. 36.

are ready for you. You won't need your parachutes, for you can just walk down on the flak." This propaganda had been going on all the time. Many rumors spread throughout the Marshalling Area. "Old men, women, and children have been trained to maim or poison members of the invading army." "Sharpened sticks have been set up to run us through as we land." "Wide areas have been wired to detonate when the landings are made." "Would the enemy use poison gas on us as a last desperate effort to save the homeland? We have no gas masks with us!"[137] We really didn't pay attention, but we did know that they knew when and where we were coming. Contrary to the propagandists' aims, this news actually boosted our morale, getting us even more agitated and ready to fight. Many men of the 17th got Mohawk (scalplock) haircuts to match the propaganda's expectations of U.S. Paratroopers. German propaganda reports claimed that "American paratroopers were a bunch of murderers who had had to kill their mothers and fathers before being allowed to join the paratroopers and who could be identified by their Indian-style haircuts."[138] So to meet the German's expectations, many opted for the American Indian look.

Although the general news of U.S. airborne plans were in German hands, many precautions were still taken in our encampment. As we became aware of our destiny, or at least of the next day's plans, extra guards were placed around the Marshalling Area so that no one could leave or escape.

We were treated well while we bivouacked in the Marshalling Area. No one had their duties to pull and large tents had already been set up for us, and for once, the 464th cooks did not have to prepare any meals. We were offered anything we wanted to eat. Steak, turkey, pancakes – anything within reason was available. If I correctly recall, I had steak. I also wrote a letter home to be mailed, so we were told, after the drop. This was the first time during the war that soldiers were allowed to say where they were going and not have those passages snipped out by censors.[139] Soldiers who had not previously completed a form will were encouraged to do so, and Army officials pledged to hold them on our

---

[137] John F Magill, a Forward Observer in the 466th PFAB, recalled these rumors in his <u>We Led From The Sky</u>.

[138] Ross, <u>Sky Men</u>, p. 281.

[139] Crookenden, <u>Airborne at War</u>, p. 97.

behalf. We were also reminded to sign up for the $10,000 life insurance policy if we had not done so. However, we troopers knew that packing our chutes correctly was really our best life insurance. Wade Hinson in our battalion recalls being called upon to help load equipment into the C-47s the night before our jump.[140] In most instances, every trooper was left to himself. Most men spent their time checking and rechecking their supplies and equipment. And, as proud paratroopers, we also polished our boots.

The weather forecast was favorable, and following Lieutenant General Lewis H. Brereton's recommendation, Field Marshal Sir Bernard L. Montgomery had announced to the upper brass before 1700 that the operation would proceed the next day as planned. "On the 7th February I told you we were going into the ring for a final and last round; there would be no time limit: we would continue fighting until our opponent is knocked out . . . . And having crossed the Rhine, we will crack about in the plains of Northern Germany, chasing the enemy from pillar to post . . . . Over the Rhine, then, let us go. And good hunting to you all on the other side."[141]

We were aroused on the morning of March 24, our D-Day, to reveille blown at 0300, much earlier than usual. Many had not slept much that night anyway. What thoughts had passed through their minds, keeping them awake, are known but to them and to God. Although prayers were usually offered en masse before breakfast, this morning's prayers seemed extra special. Chaplains from various denominations led prayer sessions, the Catholic priest heard Confessions and offered Absolution and Extreme Unction.

Unlike our previous mess tents where batteries of 100 men typically ate together, here in Chalons, several hundred gathered together in massive mess tents for our meals. Breakfast was plentiful, and the aroma of steaks filled the air. In American tradition, we even had apple pie. William Pandak of the 464th reported that when he and John Charette

---

[140] Wade C. Hinson to Robert L. Wilson, December 13, 2003.

[141] "Colonel E.S. Branigan is Awarded the Legion of Merit for Initiative," article clipping from unnamed periodical, February 1946, p. 15, William B. Breuer Papers, Box 3, World War II Units 17th Airborne Division, "Rhine River Crossing. 17th ABN Div.," Folder, USAMHI, and a shorter version reprinted in Pimlott, "Crossing the Rhine," p. 141.

left for the mess tent, they were surprised that "they had everything" laid out before them. Some of our boys had a hearty meal. Some toyed with their food. Some ate hardly anything. Pandak noted "It was like our last meal." Ross Carter thought of the irony underlying the phrase: "The condemned man ate hearty."[142] Just like the night before, it was difficult to know what anyone else was thinking about. Some had worried themselves sick.

Leaving the mess hall, there was a long table laid out with boxes of cigarettes, candy, and gum. Pandak took a carton of cigarettes, Charette took boxes of each. After they got back to their tent, Pandak laughed and told Charette, "You got all that stuff – where [are] you going to carry them?" So as "we put our . . . equipment on," Charette recalls that they "left them on the cot for whoever [would] use the tent next."[143]

We had our equipment with us in the Marshalling Area. We wore our jump suits over our long johns, and we were heavily laden with equipment. The "riggers," wing-wearing paratroopers who cared for and packed our chutes, had sewn extra pockets on some people's outfits so that they, the machine gunners, for instance, might carry extra parts for their weaponry on their bodies.[144] I put on my combat boots and packed an extra pair of socks in my musette bag – that bag which most soldiers carried on their back but which troopers wore in front under their reserve parachute, at least until they got rid of their chute after landing. I also packed leather gloves that had a warm woolen liner, but I was planning to jump bear-handed. My mess kit, pup tent/poncho, blanket, some extra carbine ammunition, at least a couple of folding packets of toilet paper, razor, Zippo lighter, hygienic "cleaning patches," and K-rations for three days were also stashed away in my musette bag.

---

[142] Carter, <u>Devils in Baggy Pants</u>, p. 23.

[143] Pandak, Bill to William B. Breuer (n.d.), p. 1, William B. Breuer Papers, Box 3. "Correspondence with Veterans of Division Artillery, 17th Airborne Division" Folder, USAMHI.

[144] Our riggers were paratroopers, but they did not jump with us. Instead, they were trucked in later to pick up the canopies, reserves, and other parachute parts from the battle ground.

Master Sergeant William Smithy Teaching Chute Packing, Ft. Benning, 1943

I put on my watch, filled my canteen and clipped it, as well as my M3 trench knife, folding shovel ("trenching tool") and M-4 bayonet in its scabbard onto my belt. I also attached my first aid kit (containing a one-shot morphine syrette, "sulfa" – sulfanilamide – powder, eight anti-infection sulfadiazine tablets, a "Carlisle" or "shell" compress bandage, and a web cloth tourniquet) to my belt hook. Some in the

17th Airborne taped their first aid kits to their boot or, more commonly, to the front of their helmets. Doing so would have obscured any helmet ranking marks of the officers, thereby shielding them even further from snipers. I grabbed several handfuls of M1 grenades, filling my jump pants pockets with them and clipping a few extra onto my belt. As it was a daytime jump, we were not given flashlights. Finally, I checked to see that my spring-activated M2 paratrooper's switchblade pocket knife was secured in the easily reachable zippered lapel pocket of my M42 jump jacket. We had all heard the tales of troopers who found these knives to be lifesavers when they needed to cut themselves free from their chutes. Our switchblade pockets had two zippers, one easily reachable with the right hand and the other with the left.[145]

Pfc. Wilson with M-1 A-1 Airborne Folding Stock Carbine Rifle

I loaded my 0.30 caliber M-1 A-1 folding stock carbine rifle and clipped its scabbard to my belt. The folding stock had been introduced for airborne troops in 1942 to prevent the injuries that previous

---

[145] Gregory, <u>United States Airborne Forces</u>, p. 26.

paratroopers had received from the butt of the M-1 rifle stock knocking them under their chin or aside of their head as they were jerked about by their chutes on their descents. I carried as many extra packets of carbine shells as would fit in my pockets. Officers also added their pistols, binoculars, silk surveillance maps, and compasses to their load of gear. I left the remainder of my belongings, including my Class A uniform, my M1943 olive drab heavy field uniform, and my jump boots, in my duffle bag in our tent. I hoped that these belongings would catch up with me later via the service trucks somewhere on German soil.

We no longer used the British-developed "leg bags" or "kit bags" to carry extra equipment. Members of the 101st and 82nd Divisions had used them earlier, but they found them to be overly cumbersome, ineffective, and even dangerous during the June 1944 invasion of Normandy. Far too many of the leg bags detached themselves during the jump and were never recovered on the ground.

For the time being, everything I thought that I would need was stored as part of the nearly 75 pounds of weight that I'd have on me as I jumped from the plane. The paratrooper was the "heaviest loaded soldier in the Army," and at this moment I truly felt it.[146] Everything about us made us look just as we were marked – "U.S." – we were a force to be feared.

As Pandak and Charette were getting ready to board the plane, they heard a shot in the next tent. "We ran there and the mail clerk said he accidentally pulled the trigger of the folding stock carbine while putting in the [scabbard]. (We were instructed not to load the chamber)." So the mail clerk didn't jump that day. Pandak related that he, himself, could have "got out of the jump [because] I burned my eyelid, lips, forehead, [and] even the hair up my nose lighting the stove the day before. But I wanted to jump after all that training."[147]

After we picked up and loaded all of our equipment, we boarded a truck and were hauled to the airfield. Most of the 464th was sent to departure field A-80. However, the glider elements of the 464th,

---

[146] Bradley and Wood, <u>Paratrooper</u>, no pagination. As a point of comparison, British troopers (the "Red Devils") were not, in general, quite as heavily laden with supplies as their U.S. counterparts.

[147] Pandak, pp. 1-2.

including one officer, 42 jumpers, 10-¼ ton trucks and 4-½ ton trailers were sent to departure field A-29, where they were to leave with the 680th Glider Field Artillery Battalion.[148]

17th Airborne Division Troopers Assemble by C-46s, March 24, 1945

The Army Air Forces had established an Air Transport Command late in 1942 at Short Field near Indianapolis, Indiana. There, under the command of Col. Fred C. Borum, pilots were trained to "fly the aircraft and gliders used by the airborne troops."[149] Later, Laurinburg-Maxton Army Air Base in North Carolina became the center for most of the

---

[148] Edward S. Branigan, Jr., "Operation Varsity Airborne Phase," May 3, 1945, p. 4.

[149] B. Gregory, <u>United States Airborne Forces</u>, p. 28. According to R.E. Bilstein, Ford Motors, Waco, and Cessna produced most of the gliders. However, companies other than motor and aircraft companies including Anheuser-Busch, Gibson Refrigerators, Steinway Piano, and H.J. Heinz Pickle Company produced them, too (<u>Airlift and Airborne Operations in World War II</u>, p. 25).

10,000 U.S. gliderists trained during the war. Although a gliderist (or "glider rider" in the words of a popular song or a "Herman, no motor" according to the troopers) was part of the airborne, unlike a trooper, the gliderist had not volunteered for this duty nor did he, until June 1944, receive hazardous duty pay equal to that of a trooper.[150] One early WWII sign read "Join the Glider Troops! No Flight Pay, No Jump Pay, but Never a Dull Moment!"[151]

A glider was equipped to carry either fifteen troopers with a pilot and a co-pilot or a quarter-ton jeep or a .75 mm howitzer and its crew. In this way, gliders were even more efficient than paratroopers in delivering a "larger number of soldiers into a smaller perimeter as a more cohesive fighting force."[152] However, glider riding was not as carefree as it might appear. The "free flight" at the end of a tether attached to a tow plane demanded "constant attention" from the glider pilot guiding his airship in the plane's wake. At the end of the journey, glider landings were, at best, a "controlled crash."[153] The journalist Walter Cronkite, who rode a glider into combat in 1944, later characterized this experience as "a lifetime cure for constipation."[154]

Rows of C-47s with Waco Gliders Along Side

[150] B. Gregory, <u>United States Airborne Forces</u>, p. 29.

[151] S. Garrett, "Airborne through the Ages," p. 36.

[152] R.E. Bilstein, <u>Airlift and Airborne Operations in World War II</u>, p. 24.

[153] R.E. Bilstein, <u>Airlift and Airborne Operations in World War II</u>, pp. 25-26. That small "cone of safe tethered flight" between the tower and the 'towee' was known as the "angle of the dangle."

[154] R.E. Bilstein, <u>Airlift and Airborne Operations in World War II</u>, p. 24.

Gliders as well as the transport planes had been assembled before the troopers arrived on the airfield. When I got out of the truck at the airfield, all I could see were C-47 planes parked next to each other for seemingly a mile or more. There we picked up our main and reserve chutes that were awaiting our arrival in stacks, and we adjusted them to fit using the help of a partner in our stick. Not being rushed for time, we took up to thirty minutes to get the harness and pack adjusted just right. We boarded the plane fully loaded, wearing all of our equipment and gear.

17th Airborne Artillerymen Fitting Chutes, March 24, 1945

It was now around 0700 hours. Those in charge knew that we had some 500-600 miles to fly before reaching our DZ. We waddled up an incline into the plane planting each footstep securely and helping our brothers as they weaved under the weight of their gear. Others had to board their planes from a suspended ladder or "loading apron" hanging out of the plane's door. Once inside the plane, we identified our place in the stick, and could then take off enough of our equipment so that we might relax – relax at least from a lessening of the weight. Still, even with our equipment off, we were snuggly packed together.

En route to the Rhine, March 24, 1945

"The first element of parachute troops, the 507th Combat Team took off [beginning at 0717], followed rapidly by the remainder of the Division."[155] The 507th Combat Team, some 2100 infantry and 379 artillerymen, filled 181 Gooney Birds.[156] Up here, on this flight, we were truly banded together. Rank mattered much less up here; everyone was just the same as the other. Wondering thoughts filled our

---

[155] "Historical Report of Operation Varsity," p. 1.

[156] C. Blair, <u>Ridgway's Paratroopers</u>, p.453, and N. Crookenden, <u>Airborne at War</u>, p. 103.

heads. "Was this trip really necessary?" We brothers were cordial with each other that morning, at times telling each other anything we felt that we needed to say as we were awaiting our jump. Some of the men in my stick were just not very talkative that morning. We were not interrupted by the pilot's radio static as radio silence was maintained throughout this flight.[157] From what I recall, I walked around and talked to as many of my brothers and said as much as anyone else did that morning. Normally, I was not such a talkative chap, but this must have been my way of releasing tension that morning. I'd also look out of the window or the open door and walk around a bit more – though you must realize, there were not too many places that we could go. We had to remember that the floor and the sides of the path inside that Gooney Bird were full of equipment bags, so we all had to carefully watch our step.

On the flight, I was somewhat frightened knowing that now I was really going to war – something that I had never before directly encountered. We knew the casualties would likely be high. It could just as easily be me as the next guy. But I also knew that casualties were not always, or even often, fatalities. I saw no rational reason to think that I was not coming home. I just assumed that I was going to get through the combat ahead. When some in our stick voiced concern that this might be their last flight, our stick leader quickly quelled such matters.

Aboard the plane we were told that our "P-Hour," the troopers' drop hour, would be 1000 hours that morning. It was confirmed during the flight that our destination was Wesel. We knew that they knew we were coming. We also believed that they knew our point of attack. Our stick leader warned us that we were likely to encounter considerable flak. He quipped, "When you step out the door of the plane and you walk out about ten feet before you start to fall, then you know that the flak is awfully heavy."

Flying on March 24 as part of the IX Troop Carrier Command were thirteen war correspondents, including Edward R. Murrow, who had assembled to cover this spectacular event. They represented media sources including the <u>New York Times</u>, the <u>Chicago Tribune</u>, the

---

[157] "Field Order No. 5 for Operation Varsity," Headquarters IX Troop Carrier Command U.S. Army Air Forces, March 16, 1945, p. 6.

Mutual Broadcasting Company, the National Editorial Association, Associated Press, the <u>Air Force Magazine</u>, the French News Service, <u>Stars and Stripes</u>, and the Columbia Broadcasting System (CBS).[158]

In the words of CBS reporter Richard C. Hottelet, flying in a silver B-17 Flying Fortress full of combat cameramen and reporters alongside the troop carrying planes, the weather "was on our side. For eleven superb days the sun had crossed the sky, brilliant from the moment it rose to its last setting red. It helped the men patrolling the sky, and the bomber fleets that went out day after day and night after night. It helped the men on the ground by drying out the soil over which they would have to move."[159] It was a clear and sunny morning, just as Montgomery and his command team had anticipated based upon their preparations made in accordance with weather charts a month earlier.

Planning for Operation Varsity began on March 9 when Field Marshal Montgomery issued orders for a Rhine crossing north of the Ruhr industrial land of Germany's Westphalia region. This Operation's key personnel, all of whom worked under Montgomery's command, included Lieutenant General Sir Miles Dempsey (2nd British Army), Lieutenant General Lewis H. Brereton (1st Allied Airborne Army, in charge of timing the airborne attack, based largely on weather forecasts), Major General Matthew B. Ridgway (XVIII Corps), Major General Richard H. Gale (XVIII Corps, who with General Ridgway commanded the airborne task force), Lieutenant General Evelyn H. Barker (8th British Corps), Lieutenant General Neil Ritchie (12th British Corps), Major General Frederick L. Anderson (8th Bomber Command), Major General Paul L. Williams (IX Troop Carrier Command, who arranged troop carrying needs for both U.S. and British forces), Major General William M. Miley (17th U.S. Airborne Division), Major General Eric L. Bols (6th British Airborne Division), Brigadier W.D.C. Greenacre (6th Guards Armored Brigade), Brigadier Derek Mills-Roberts (1st Commando Brigade), and Lieutenant Colonel Brian Forster Mortan Franks (SAS Ground Force).

---

[158] Howard K. Smith and Eric Sevareid were among the correspondents covering Operation Plunder the night before Varsity.

[159] Richard C. Hottelet, "Big Jump into Germany," <u>Collier's</u>, May 5, 1945, as reprinted in <u>Reporting World War II. Part II: American Journalism, 1944-1946</u> (New York: The Library of America, 1995), p. 650.

Montgomery's intentions were "to secure a bridgehead prior to developing operations to isolate the Ruhr and to thrust into the northern plains of Germany" en route to Berlin.[160] British commanders flew from Netheravon to meet their American counterparts at Chalons on March 17. Several weeks prior to the actual airborne assault, Montgomery would instigate an air barrage to "pummel the area" along an eleven-mile front south of Wesel and the Lippe River, concentrated on destroying rail yards, bridges, communication centers, and industrial sites.[161] It was clear to many in command and in the ranks that the Rhine crossing presented the "biggest military challenge since Normandy."[162]

Arnhem remained a dark shadow over Montgomery and over American forces, too. After paratroopers had been dropped at different points into Arnhem, they had to endure long marches before encountering the enemy, thereby giving the opposition plenty of time to organize after the airborne assault.[163] This plan would not be repeated in the Ruhr. The drop would be concentrated and "would go in on one enormous airlift as quickly as technical considerations allowed." Still, the crossing had its complexity. The hard winter of 1944-45 had created such flooding along its path that, as John Pimlott argued, it was "sure to hamper Allied progress" in any Rhine crossing attempt.[164] Montgomery's plan was to close in along the Rhine all along its length to prevent any German stronghold from being secured on its west bank. As in any war, fortune also played its hand. Hitler unknowingly eased Montgomery's plan, albeit slightly, when on March 21, with "bitter reluctance," he consented to having his 7th Army withdraw from the west to the east banks of the Rhine.

---

[160] Peter Allen, <u>One More River: The Rhine Crossings of 1945</u> (New York: Charles Scribner's Sons, 1980), p. 209.

[161] Flanagan, <u>Airborne: A Combat History of American Airborne Forces</u>, p. 289.

[162] Allen, <u>One More River</u>, p. 223.

[163] For a critical assessment of the Arnhem Campaign, see Frank Steer, <u>Arnhem: The Fight to Sustain: The Untold Story of the Airborne Logisticians</u> (Barnsley, U.K.: Pen & Sword, 2001), Donald R. Burgett, <u>Road to Arnhem: A Screaming Eagle in Holland</u> (New York: Dell, 2001), Robert Peatling, <u>Without Tradition: 2 Para, 1941-1945</u> (Barnsley, U.K.: Pen and Sword, 2004), and Cornelius Ryan's gripping, <u>A Bridge Too Far</u> (New York: Simon & Schuster, 1974).

[164] Pimlott, "Crossing the Rhine," p. 129.

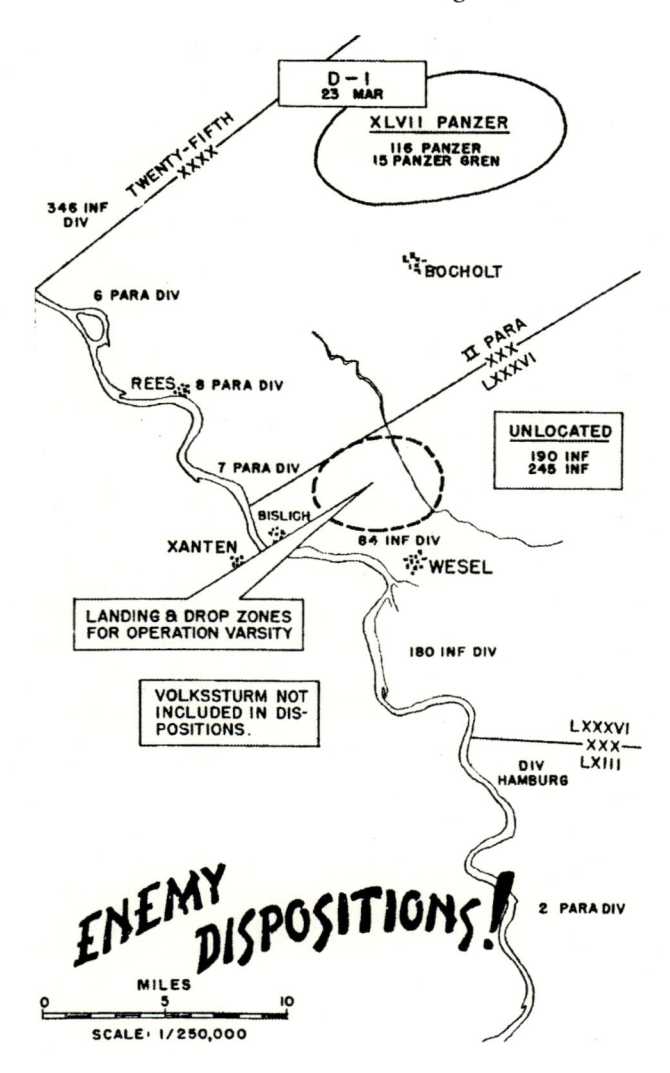

Still, Montgomery knew that the German defenses held strong. By March 21, his Intelligence Staff had identified "12 German divisions across the entire frontage of [the] 21st Army Group." These divisions represented some 50,000 troops plus 35,000 *Volkssturm* – the "elder soldiers and civilians of all ages" who had been hastily outfitted with uniforms, or at least armbands bearing the words *Deutscher Volkssturm* and *Wehrmacht* and any available weapons.[165] Their armamentarium

---

[165] Hickey, <u>Out of the Sky</u>, p. 178.

consisted of rifles, pistols, machine carbines, grenades, hunting knives, anti-tank weapons, Mgs (Metal Gear Solids), mortars, light flak weapons, mines, and explosives. Although known to have "fought with valor" in the east of Germany, here in the west, they "have only half heartedly attempted to do their assigned task." By this point of the war, it was reputed that the *Volkssturm* would "surrender at the first opportunity." Still, "this type of soldier" was known to be "treacherous" and "must be treated accordingly."[166]

At least two Panzer Divisions, the 116th Panzer and the 15th Panzergrenadiers, with "100 tanks and self propelled guns" were also known to be close by.[167] And, of Germany's remaining 1285 aircraft, some 850 were accessible to northwestern Germany at this time.[168] Thus, the anticipated German defenses were not to be taken lightly.

We had heard that allied troops had bombarded with a saturation bombing the area of our destination very heavily for nearly 3 days before we jumped. Some 3000 aircraft and 2000 bombers had flown in missions in order to accomplish this objective.[169] In Army language, this effort was "expected to neutralize or render ineffective a considerable portion of potential enemy ground defenses."[170] In addition to the casualties inflicted by these assaults, "it cannot be doubted," General Eisenhower later argued, "that they produced a serious moral effect upon the enemy, who, after enduring three days of unremitting hell from the air, were in no condition to meet the frontal assault when it was launched."[171]

While in the air on the morning of March 24, we saw other planes, many of them pulling gliders, but we had no idea of the grandiose airhead formation that was being formed. Stories commonly recount the use of C-46 planes, which were bigger and could fly as fast as 260 mph, as the new model of troop carriers that particular day.[172] The

---

[166] "Field Order No. 5 for Operation Varsity," Annex No.1, p. 11.

[167] "USAF Airborne Operations. World War II and Korean War," USAF Historical Division Liaison Office, March 1962, p. 81.

[168] "Field Order No. 5 for Operation Varsity," Annex No.1, p. 7.

[169] Crookenden, Airborne at War, p. 96.

[170] "Field Order No. 5 for Operation Varsity," Annex No.1, p. 13.

[171] General of the Army, "Supreme Commanders Dispatch for Operations in Northwest Europe, 6 June 1944 – 8 May 1945," pp. 94-95.

[172] Bilstein, Airlift and Airborne Operations in World War II, p. 18.

C-46 planes, with their distinctive 'double bubble' fuselage, carried twice as many troopers since they had exit doors on both sides of the plane. Thus, by using the C-46s, more men could "land closer together and, therefore, assemble faster" at their DZs.[173] Afterall, the "weakest link" in airborne operations thus far had been the "assembly time upon landing."[174] To their credit, these planes also held much more fuel, thereby allowing more of them to reach and return from target zones that were hundreds of miles away. Their fuel range of 3000 miles was twice that of the C-47s.[175]

However, pilots reported that the C-46s were temperamental to fly, and they had difficulty in maintaining their place in formation, particularly when needing to slow down as they approached their respective glider LZs (landing zones) and paratrooper DZs. A more critical concern was to be found in their design. Unlike the C-47, that had "been fitted with plasticized 'self-sealing' fuel tanks," the gas and hydraulic lines of the C-46s had no protection against enemy fire.[176] If a wing tank was punctured, its fuel "ran down into the fuselage, and another strike would set it ablaze in a second."[177] Due to this faulty design, this plane quickly became nicknamed the "flying coffin." Indeed, after the difficulties encountered by these planes during the Operation Varsity attack, the C-46 planes were never again used in an airborne assault.

---

[173] Ross, The Skymen, p. 264.

[174] Mitchell, "Epilogue. One Last Great Jump," p. 263.

[175] Bilstein, Airlift and Airborne Operations in World War II, p. 18.

[176] Blair, Ridgway's Paratroopers, p. 457.

[177] Weeks, Airborne Equipment, p. 106. Originally named the "Condor," the C-46s had been renamed the "Commando" by the time of Operation Varsity.

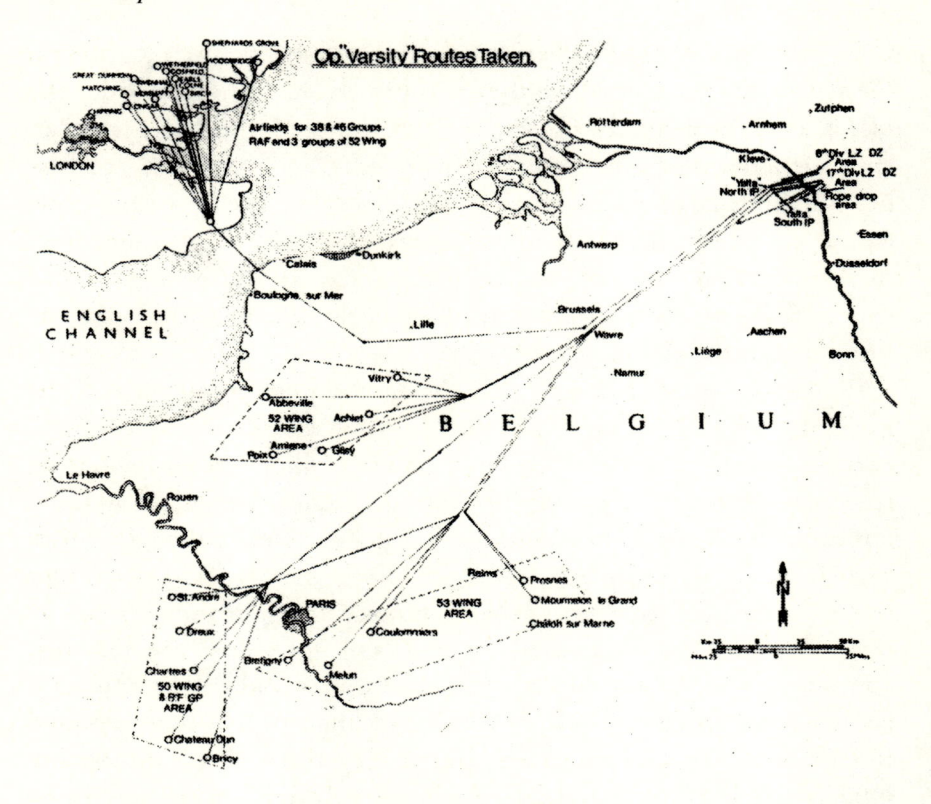

Though not visible by us, our plane had joined a large armada of planes originating from 17 airfields in France bounded by the cities of Amiens, Orléans, and Evereux, and 11 airfields in the East Anglian area of England, all of which rendezvoused over Wavre, Belgium, just above the 1815 battlefield of Waterloo. From that point on, the planes originating from France flew into the right stream, whereas those from England flew into the left; each of us surrounding a center stream of glider serials.[178] A literal "sky train" of two and one-half hours in length (or air space) flew as part of the 226 C-47s and 72 C-46s carrying 17,122 paratroopers together with 906 gliders being pulled by 610 C-47 tow planes (314 single tow and 296 double tow).[179] This "sky

---

[178] "Field Order No. 5 for Operation Varsity," p. 2.

[179] "Historical Report of Operation Varsity," p. 1. For the "first time in combat," the IXth Troop Carrier Command utilized double glider tow – and it proved "very successful." "Narrative of Operation Varsity," p. 7. Later accounts discuss slightly different numbers of carriers and troopers. For instance, three reliable secondary

train" included 676 U.S. fighter escort planes as well as 213 British fighter planes, bringing the number to nearly 5000 planes total.[180] The use of fighter planes to protect our unarmed transport carriers was critical for the success of the mission. In addition to the C-47s and C-46s, this "sky transport armada" included R.A.F. converted Armstrong Whitworth Albemares, Handley Page Halifaxes, Short Stirlings, Waco CG-4As, Airspeed Horsas and General Aircraft Hamilcars.[181] This wide assortment of aircraft appeared, as CBS reporter Hottelet picturesquely described, as a "mighty olive-green river" in the sky that "surged steadily," intent on proving to be a "mightier river than the German Rhine."[182]

As we got close to the Rhine, we could tell that the sun-filled portion of our flight was through. The birds seemed to have had more sense that we did at the moment for they were long gone from this area. Here, as Hottelet described, "there was no sunlight; here in the center of green and fertile land was a clearly marked area of death. The smoke seemed a shroud. Outlines below us were indistinct. What had seemed warm now appeared ominously cold, and almost clammy."[183]

Unbeknownst to us that morning, smoke had actually covered much of the area for several days. Initially, Field Marshal Montgomery had screened his build up of ground troops on the west of the Rhine with "an extensive use of smoke on a fifty mile front."[184] Operation Plunder, the amphibious part of this attack, was initiated at 2000

---

sources describe a skytrain of 1,696 transport aircraft plus 1348 gliders landing a total of 21,680 troopers. Bilstein, Airlift and Airborne Operations in World War II, p. 37, Gregory, United States Airborne Forces, p. 121, and Mike Verier, 82nd Airborne Division "All American," Spearhead volume 4 (Hersham, Surrey: Ian Allan, 2001), p. 59. Clair in Ridgway's Paratroopers (p. 455) noted that the U.S. component of this skytrain numbered some 4, 946 paratroopers and 4,613 gliderists. For an overview of ETO paratroop transport in Varsity and other operations, see H. Rex Sharma, Pulse and Repulse: Troop Carrier and Airborne Teams in Europe during World War II (Austin, TX: Eakin, 1995).

[180] Bart Hagerman, "Operation Varsity: The Airborne Assault over the Rhine," in Bart Hagerman (ed) U.S.A. Airborne 50th Anniversary, 1940-1990 (Paducah, KY: Turner Publishing Co., 1990), p. 133.

[181] Gregory, United States Airborne Forces, pp. 121-122.

[182] Hottelet, "Big Jump into Germany," p. 652.

[183] Hottelet, "Big Jump into Germany," p. 652.

[184] "Narrative of Operation Varsity," p. 5.

hours on March 23. Following an hour-long intensive artillery barrage running from the eastern Rhine banks through the anticipated DZs and LZs, considerable movement occurred in crossing the Rhine at three points along its northern end. The 2nd Army, under Lt. Gen. Dempsey, crossed along a 20km (twelve-mile) front, between the cities of Xanteen and Rees, with the Canadian 1st Army in the rear. This first wave across the Rhine used armored amphibious vehicles and tanks fitted with flotation devices. There were no serious setbacks, and by dawn, "nine small bridgeheads had been secured across the Rhine" in the greater Emmerich-Wesel area.[185]

---

[185] "Narrative of Operation Varsity," pp. 6-7. Crookenden recounts the sequence of events in Airborne at War, p. 97, as does Winston G. Ramsey in "Operation Plunder," in After the Battle, No. 16 (London: Battle of Britain Prints International, Ltd, 1977), pp. 15-27. From engineering perspectives, see Frank E. Stevenson, "Third Army's Planning for the Crossing of the Rhine River," Military Review 30 (1951): 33-42, Barry W. Fowle, "The Rhine River Crossings," in Barry W. Fowle (ed) Builders and Fighters: U.S. Army Engineers in World War II (Fort Belvoir, Virginia: Office of History, United States Army Corps of Engineers, 1992), pp. 463-475, as well as Alexander McKee's The Race for the Rhine Bridges (NY: Stein and Day, 1971). Charles Whiting focused upon the British Army's push to cross the Rhine in his Bounce the Rhine (Havertown, PA: Casemate, 2002).

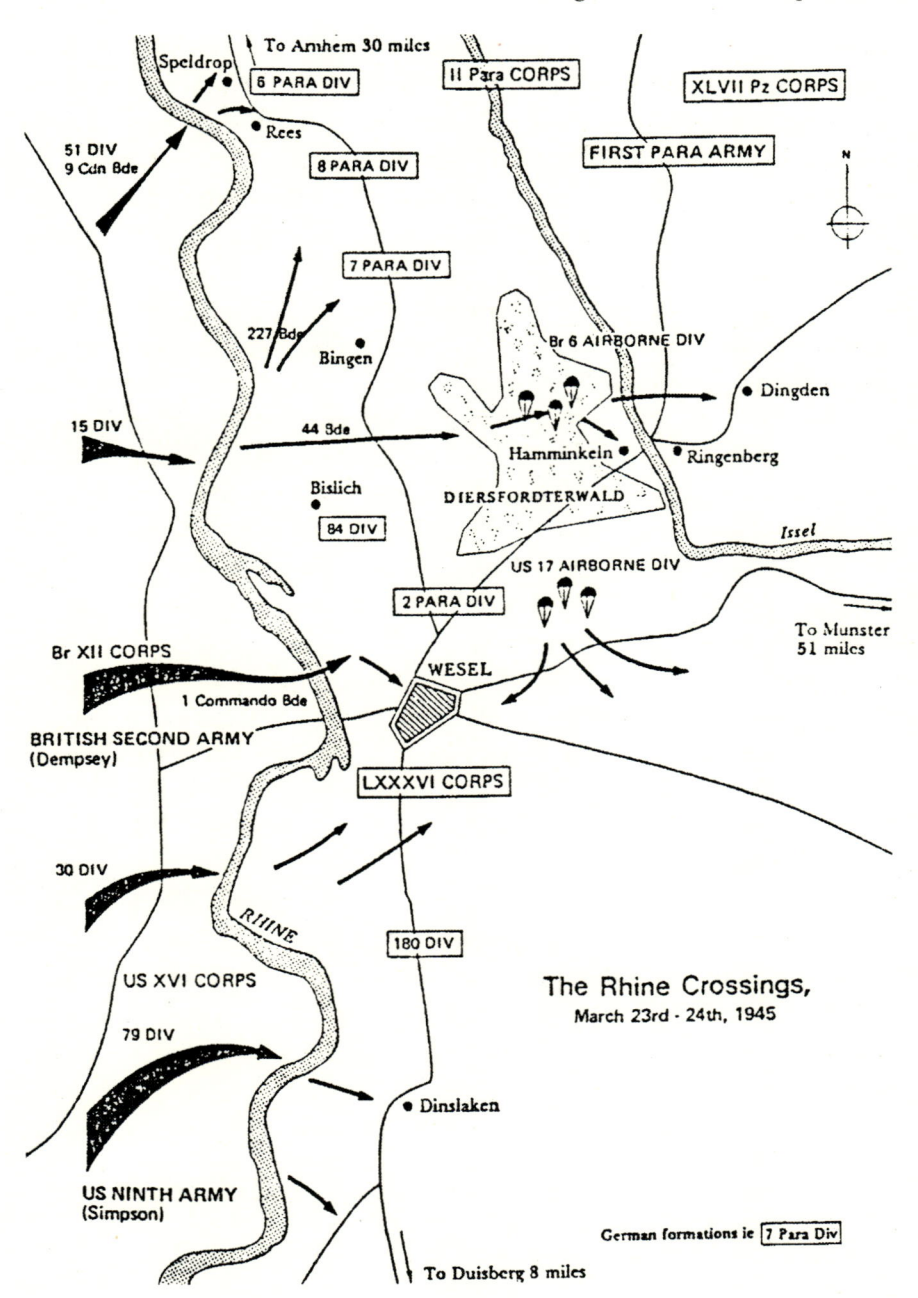

The Rhine Crossings,
March 23rd - 24th, 1945

German formations ie 7 Para Div

The idea of initiating water crossings before the airborne attack
– the reversal of previous operations – was anticipated to surprise the
Germans.[186] It was hoped that this river assault would force the German

121

commander of the area to either "meet the seaborne landings with all forces at his disposal" or to "meet the seaborne assault with part of his strength and keep his main effort in reserve to give him enough time to see where the main attack" would be centered.[187] As the Germans were anticipating an airborne attack, it was "more likely that they would keep their main strength back of the Issel River, with only a holding force in the wood[s]."[188]

Having already gathered a mass of engineering supplies to build bridges as well as assault boats to ferry across troops and weapons, Lieutenant General George S. Patton, together with Lieutenant General Manton S. Eddy, decided to cross the Rhine some 10 miles south of Mainz, the site where the Germans anticipated that a crossing would be attempted. This new point, the village of Oppenheim, proved an excellent choice for Patton as "there was a small barge harbour which could be reached from the village but which could not be seen from across the Rhine."[189] However, to keep the enemy guessing, Patton continued to lay a heavy smoke screen at Mainz.

Around 2000 hours on the evening of March 22, twenty-four hours prior to the initiation of Operation Plunder, "without benefit of aerial bombardment, ground smoke, artillery preparations or airborne resistance" at the site, Patton's Third Army crossed the Rhine. He had upheld his pledge to ensure that U.S. forces crossed the Rhine before those of Montogmery.

Thirty six hours later, 1000 hours on Saturday, March 24, the P-Hour of our D-Day, the Rhine came into view on our plane.[190] Montgomery's air artillery bombardment had been ordered to cease fire by the time our plane reached the Rhine. We could see the smoke and shattered trees, many of which were still afire or smoldering. Some

---

[186] William C. Mitchell, "Epilogue. One Last Great Jump: Operation Varsity," in Kurt Gable, <u>Making of a Paratrooper,</u> p. 257.

[187] "Field Order No. 5 for Operation Varsity," Annex No.1, p. 11.

[188] "ASAF Airborne Operations," p. 81.

[189] P. Allen, <u>One More River,</u> p. 231.

[190] The "Historical Report of Operation Varsity" notes on p. 2 that the 464th PFAB dropped at 1008, some 15 minutes after the very first men of the 507th Combat Team had landed. March 24 was also the date of Operation Rype in which 20 troopers of the Office of Strategic Services (OSS) Norwegian Special Operations Group (NORSO) jumped at Jaevsjo, Norway to aid the resistance.

of the smoke we saw had originated from the smoke grenades that the Army Air Corps had dropped and the Pathfinders had placed to signify specific DZs. The Pathfinders were the heavily laden specialists (often referred to as the "Suicide Squad") who dropped an hour or so in advance of the main airborne assault to prepare the groundwork "in accordance with Signal Communications" for the force that followed.[191] In some drops, the Pathfinders included demolition experts who cleared massive areas of landmines before the airborne onslaught. For night drops, they set up Halifane lights. For our drop, they set up Eureka radar sets to establish earth-bound radio signals. Seasoned Pathfinder, Colonel Joel Crouch led the Troop Carrier Pathfinder Group for the 17th Division taking off ahead of our plane from Chartres.

The first four serials to liftoff from our airfield earlier that morning were Crouch's lead serial of 46 aircraft carrying the 507th 1st Battalion commanded by Paul F. Smith. Following it was a serial with Charles Timmes' 2nd Battalion, another serial with Allen W. Taylor's 3rd Battalion, then the fourth serial that included Branigan's artillery.[192] Crouch's actions would ultimately indicate the precise time for turning on the Green Light.[193]

It addition to the smoke on the ground, we began to notice a lot of flak in the air, identifiable by dark puffs of smoke. With an aim to come in over our DZ between 600 and 500 feet in the air, we still had a considerable descent to make from the 1500 foot level we had been flying since France.[194] We knew that we would encounter considerably more flak in our descent.

Shrapnel and bullets from the ack-ack guns of *Generaloberst* Johannes Blaskowitz's German Army Group H on the ground hit with a pecking like noise along the bottom side of our plane. The Germans had installed "approximately 114 heavy guns and countless ground defenses" in the area that, unbeknownst to them, represented our

---

[191] "Field Order No. 5 for Operation Varsity," p. 7. For an overview of WWII Pathfinder action, see Jeff Moran, American Airborne Pathfinders in World War II (Atglen, PA: Schiffer Publishing, Ltd, 2003).

[192] Blair, Ridgway's Paratroopers, p. 454.

[193] Crookenden, Airborne at War, p. 102.

[194] "Field Order No. 5 for Operation Varsity," p. 3, recommended that we were to fly at an altitude of 1500 feet to Marfak, then lower to 1000 feet at Yalta.

precise DZs and LZs.[195] Four DZs and six LZs had been identified within an area about six miles long and five miles wide; a range that was deemed as coverable by the substantial allied artillery support already on the ground. This location provided "an unprecedented degree of concentration" for an airborne assault.[196]

We were one of three columns of three-plane V-formations (i.e., nine planes wide, a "V of Vs") flying in a compact airhead coming in over our DZs. Each column consisted of a trail of 5 planes, thereby comprising a serial of 45 aircraft. Each serial was to be spaced behind the one preceding it with a three to four minute interval of airspace.[197] We flew in the fourth serial which, together with the three preceding it, carried 2,479 troopers in 181 C-47s to DZ "W."[198] We knew that we were but one stick of thousands to make serial jumps that day, but in our plane, we felt quite alone and in a dangerous position.[199] We were absolutely ready to leave that plane by the time we reached our DZ. The amount and sound of the flak we received would have encouraged even non-troopers to prepare to jump.

It was now time to slow our previous 150 mph speed to 100 mph and begin our descent. As we descended, the pecking noise turned more to a hail like sound, and the plane, being peppered by small arms fire, was beginning to vibrate, though just slightly. The aircraft crew was fitted with flak helmets, flak vests, flak aprons over their legs, and a flak pan – or at least a steel bar – to sit on.[200] We stood up so as to become a smaller target than we had been sitting down for any flak that might come up through the floor of the plane.

---

[195] Mitchell, "Epilogue. One Last Great Jump," p. 257. For an overview of the German defense during this Rhine crossing, see Major Justin L.C. Eldridge's "Defense on the Rhine," Military Intelligence 21 (1995): 38-44, 52.

[196] "USAF Airborne Operations," p. 80.

[197] "Field Order No. 5 for Operation Varsity," p. 5.

[198] "USAF Airborne Operations," p. 86.

[199] James "Jumping Jim" Gavin, the youngest general in the Allied Armies had risen to lead the 82nd Airborne Division by the time of Operation Varsity. Although the 82nd did not fly in Varsity as they were "being saved for Berlin," Gavin did fly at about 1800 feet above the troop carrier planes that day assessing the overall assault from the sky. His description of our flight pattern seems to be among the most accurate. See Gavin, On to Berlin, p. 134.

[200] Crookenden, Airborne at War, p. 103.

We gathered more anti-aircraft fire, and the plane slowed down even further. I recall that I felt as if we were becoming much more of a sitting target – and indeed we were. Our door-less plane shook and rattled even more furiously from the flak. Pieces of shrapnel cut through the skin of the plane. It was scary. It was frightening. Anyone who would say otherwise is a damn liar. We were receiving, as was later recorded, the "heaviest flak barrage that airborne troops had encountered during the war."[201]

It was during our descent that the red light came on. By that time, we had our equipment on and were harnessed up. Theoretically, we knew we had five minutes after that signal until the time of our jump. In reality, I have no idea how long we waited as time had held little meaning to us that morning. The red light merely warned us that we were nearing Wesel. I hooked up the D-ring end of my static line to the overhead plane rail, and I checked the equipment of the trooper in front of me. Our captain was our Jumpmaster that day. We sounded off, shuffled to the door, huddled towards and stood pushing against the fellow in front of us. The head of our stick was now well positioned in the door.

---

[201] Breuer, <u>Geronimo</u>, p. 546.

Troopers in the Stick, WWII Memorial, Washington, D.C.

A river, the Rhine, a "shimmery silver strip" came into view out of our open doorway and out of our C-47's round windows. We knew that our jump was imminent.[202] We crossed the river, got some 8 to 10 miles on the other side, and the green light came on. "Okay you bastards, we are here to eradicate you." It's kill or be killed. Out we go! This "Devil in Baggy Pants" came down true to his Division's motto,

---

[202] Breuer, <u>Geronimo</u>, p. 546.

like "Thunder From Heaven."[203] According to my enemy, "Hell had been unchained, [and] the decisive major attack had begun."[204]

---

[203] The phrase "Devils in Baggy Pants," in reference to U.S. Airborne Forces, originated from the diary of a German officer who had opposed the 504th Parachute Infantry Regiment on the Anzio beachhead. It read, "American parachutists – devils in baggy pants – are less than 100 meters from my outpost line. I can't sleep at night; they pop up from nowhere and we never know when or how they strike next. Seems like the black hearted devils are everywhere . . . ." Reprinted in Carter, Devils in Baggy Pants, dedication page.

[204] Major General Heinz Fiebig, "The 84th Infantry Division During the Fights from Reichswald to Wesel," Foreign MS B-843, USAMHI.

Chapter 5:

Green Light – Jumping Across the Rhine with Operation Varsity

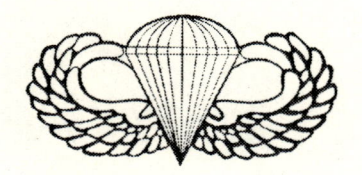

The day started early, and never really ended.

Pat Davis, Paratrooper Historian

With a rustling of gear we hooked up, checked equipment, and moved to the door. Our mouths were dry, our forehead and hands were sweaty, and somebody in the stick was vomiting. Green Light – GO! In 10 seconds, the entire stick had left the plane. Our plane, like all of those over DZ "W" made a 180º turn to the right after dropping its load and climbed up to 2500 feet as quickly as possible in order to flee the flack and return to its base station.[205]

---

[205] "Field Order No. 5 for Operation Varsity," p. 5.

Paratroopers by the hundreds were spilling out of planes in their chutes east of the Rhine River. We had been drilled for months on the five points of a parachute jump: "check your body position and count; check your canopy; keep a sharp look-out for trouble below while you are going down; prepare to land; and land, as you have been taught, and no other way."[206]

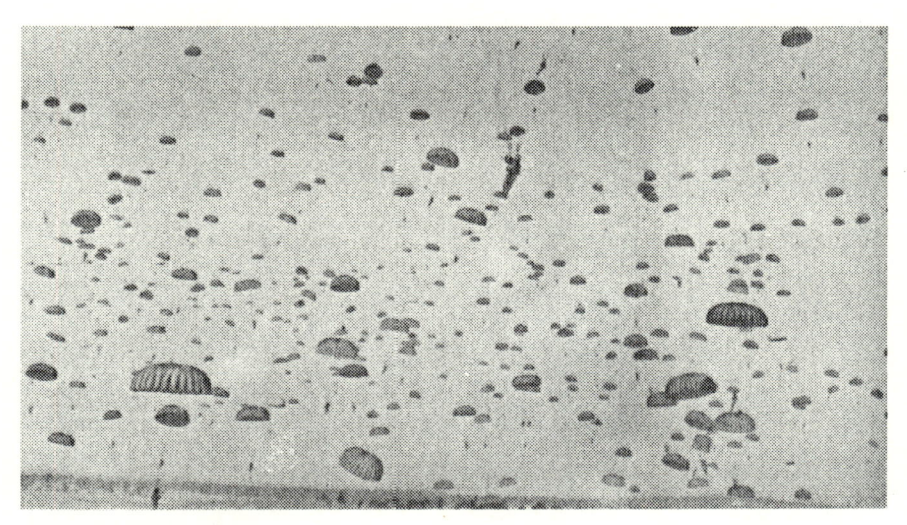

The Rhine Jump

My chute opened in three seconds, and for the next ten seconds I descended while being fired upon. Wade Hinson of the 464th felt that he was being "fired on from all directions."[207] Some troopers visibly went limp on their descent, indicating that they had been hit.

The Axis forces were well dug into the area and had, at least before the recent strafing, enjoyed a considerable canopy of natural cover from the high trees. However, by the time of our arrival, our DZs were but a crippled forest. Previously the highly wooded area, known as Diersfordter Wald, had been a German stronghold. Though "scarcely 100 feet above the river," this "high ground provided the only good natural observation points in the area, and the trees provided cover from which German artillery could rake the stream. Until the wood was

---

[206] Ayling, They Fly to Fight, p. 54.
[207] Wade C. Hinson to Robert L. Wilson, December 13, 2003.

taken, construction of bridges across the Rhine," at least at this point of its path, "would be impossible."[208] For the descending paratrooper, the remnants of trees still presented a formidable obstacle. Entangling one's chute in tree branches made a trooper an easy 'sitting duck' target for the enemy. A number of dead and dying troopers were found suspended in the trees throughout the day. Until their bodies were later cut down, they remained an ominous symbol of the danger involved in our mission. They also provoked an even greater hatred of our enemy.

Canopy Trail, Wesel, March 24, 1945

Strategic planning had worked in our favor as we had no wind force to hamper us from getting out of our parachutes.[209] Unlike the harnesses we had trained in, we had recently been issued a newly designed British harness that allowed a quicker release through pulling a pin, then turning and hitting a stomach-centered dial. Upon hitting the dial, our straps were all released, allowing us to step freely out of our harness's swing-seat or "saddle." Ideally, these connections could be released slightly before reaching hitting the ground, allowing us even greater maneuverability out of our parachute. Although this newly improved design was highly praised and no doubt helped save many soldiers, a few problems did occur with it in this battle. Some soldiers, being unfamiliar with this new device, released themselves midair and completed their fall without a parachute. Others, frustrated by this

---

[208] "USAF Airborne Operations," p. 80.
[209] Branigan later reported the wind velocity at the time of our drop as 8-10 mph.

new harness, fiddled around with the unfamiliar release mechanism just a little too long after hitting the ground, thereby making them a standing target for the enemy.

After releasing our respective chutes, two of us crawled into a six to eight foot bomb crater. Then, after a few moments of gathering our senses, we jumped out and joined several others, including an officer, and crawled some 50 yards over the "hot" ground to hide behind a bundle. Unfortunately, this bundle was one of our ammunition boxes – just where we did not want to be at that time. Still, we knew that this ammo was of no help when separated from our cannons. So we dragged it over to the parts of the howitzer lying nearby. Bullets continued to zip over us, kicking up dirt everywhere.

Our howitzers had "hit the silk," coming down in parachutes as well. The cannons had been disassembled before they were loaded; the wheels, the barrel, and the firing mechanism were connected by a daisy chain of elastic rope. This arrangement greatly eased our hunt for the pieces since they would already be somewhat connected when they hit the ground. Branigan had originated the concept of dropping linked bundles in order to accelerate their assemblage once troopers and their artillery were on the ground. "Perceiving the relative inefficiency" of existing methods of delivering "field artillery weapons and equipment from air to ground" by parachute, Branigan worked "outside of hours, using personnel of the non-divisional battalion which he commanded." To test various improved methods, he "arranged for the necessary aircraft from the Army Air Forces continuously for a year." Part of this effort improved the controlled delivery of our weapons, the 75mm pack howitzer components at regular intervals in a manner such that the components were easier to assemble. Prior methods had resulted in such a "considerable loss of equipment and weapons" that "many officers" had concluded that the "idea of parachute field artillery ... [was] impractical." Before Varsity, the Ordnance Department had adopted Branigan's "Harness, Control Pattern, M-2" as the standard procedure for delivering field artillery by airborne forces.[210]

---

[210] Information drawn from the September 24, 1945 citation Legion of Merit awarded to Branigan for this procedure. William B. Breuer Papers, Box 3, "Rhine River Crossing. World War II Units 17th Airborne Division, 17th ABN Div.," Folder, USAMHI.

On the morning of Varsity, canvas bundles of shells had been dropped in their green metal boxes, and they had to be hunted down separately. Ammunition bundles (or 'parapacks') were marked with a particular color, allowing us to more readily distinguish them from the other supply bundles. However, the constant haze of smoke from all of the firing from both sides severely limited visibility on the ground. Fortunately, we could spot others in our Division by the bright fluorescent chartreuse silk cloths tied on our backs – at least on the ones who had not lost them during their descent. These cloths aided the close support aircraft who used them to identify Allied ground forces. On the other hand, they also aided the Germans as they more clearly marked their enemy. I still have my colored cloth, and it brings back powerful memories of this moment, the point when I faced my "Baptism of Fire." When I hold this cloth, I think back on this significant moment and the places that it and I have been together.

I recall that as we scouted for ammunition to supply the gunners, every step I took over hundreds of yards in any direction was covered by shrapnel. In the early hours after landing, this groundcover made the crawling that we had to do significantly more difficult. Being inquisitive, I picked up a few pieces of that shrapnel and stowed them quickly in my musette bag. I still have these battlefield souvenirs today.

We knew that our first objective was to get our cannons together. We hoped that we would get them ready before the Germans zeroed in on us. The sounds of battle were truly ear piercing, so we had to rely upon hand signals to hustle over this way, to turn the cannon to a different angle or, with closed fist pumping upward, to hurry and assemble. Bullets continued to zip overhead, but it was great to hear them still zipping. If they are flying overhead, they will not get you. Rather, it's the bullet that you don't hear that will be the bad one.

While in the midst of battle, the passage of time is so very difficult to perceive – both then and later when trying to recall a particular sequence of events.[211] All I can say is that within a relative short period

---

[211] Ross Carter, who saw much more combat that I did as a trooper, elaborated upon the meaning of time in his <u>Devils in Baggy Pants</u>, p. 147, stating that "After one or two battles time comes to mean nothing. A day may seem longer than a week, a month or even a year." The soldier "divides time into two parts: before entering the war and after engaging in battle. The only time-point that has meaning exists in the brief intermissions between battles."

of time, we landed in our DZ, assembled as a unit, reassembled our howitzer, determined our targets, and started firing. Our main objective was to fire over the heads of our 507th Parachute Infantry force, which had landed just previous to us in their chutes that day. This enabled them to move forward more successfully as well as forcing the Germans back from their own lines. We had practiced this maneuver in Florida, but that was no comparison to the feelings of actually being under fire while attempting to clear the way for our infantry.

According to Branigan, members of the 464th were "raked by heavy machine-gun fire while we were descending in our chutes. Bullets came so close to me that, after crashing down, I found that the dispatch case I had been carrying was riddled. On landing, my artillery men began slithering over the ground under a hail of fire, and they quickly set up three .50-caliber machine guns and began firing back at the German machine gunners."[212] Branigan's "Bastards" had achieved their objective of becoming the first airborne artillery outfit to fight with its howitzers east of the Rhine River.

Assembling Howitzer in the Field

---

[212] Branigan, as quoted in Breuer, <u>Geronimo</u>, p. 547.

In Breuer's retelling of the immediate action of the 464th, upon "spotting one enemy machine gun in a farmhouse, Branigan rapidly rounded up five of his artillerymen and led them in a charge. Firing their tommy guns and rifles, Branigan and the others raced over open ground. First Sgt. Edmund L. Kissinger went past the battalion commander, pitched a grenade into the house, and keeled over dead, a bullet through the head. Branigan and the other troopers bolted inside, sprayed the rooms with tommy-gun fire, and killed or captured the Germans."[213] One fellow with whom I'd been quite close, John E. Bidwell, from Texas was also killed that day. It always tore us up to lose our mates, but we all realized the exceptional hazards that we, as paratroopers, faced due to our placement within enemy territory.

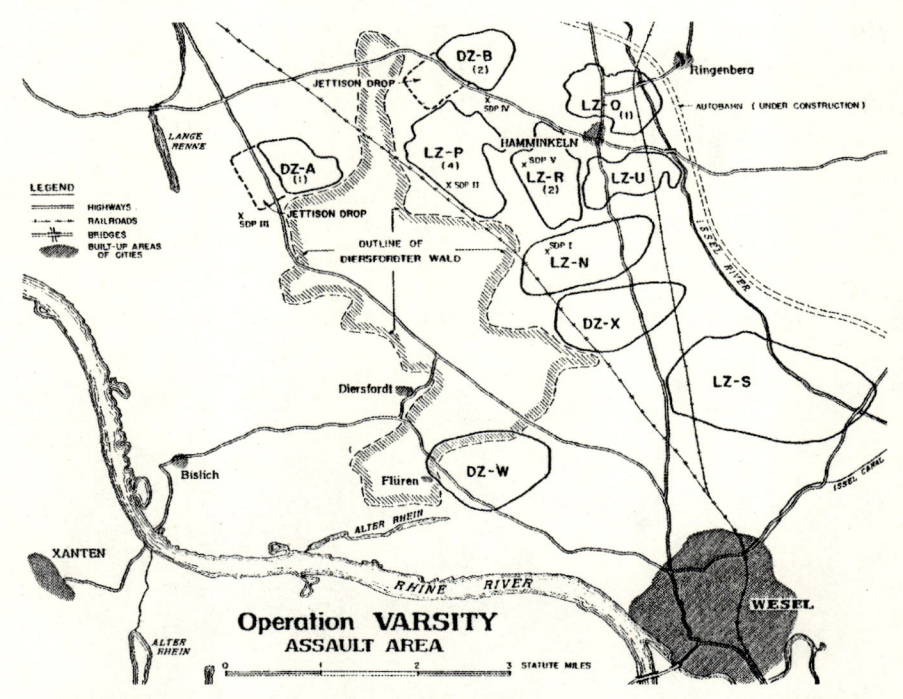

DZ "W" placed us along the southern end of the Diersfordter Wald adjacent to the village of Flüren, with the curvature of the Rhine one mile to our south and the city of Wesel, two miles to our southeast. There, we were to secure the southern part of the forest and protect the

---

[213] Branigan, as quoted in Breuer, <u>Geronimo</u> , p. 547.

right flank of the XVIII Airborne Corps. Peter Allen has summarized the geography of the Rhine at Wesel quite accurately. At Wesel, the river is "400 yards wide" between its banks; banks that extend as "winding flood plains that were inundated in winter when the river could spread for a mile or more in places. Then, when the floods subsided they left great lagoons and creeks along the shores with sand-bars that changed shape almost daily. Thus the land alongside lent itself to strong defenses in depth." The far (i.e., east) bank was "criss-crossed by a sophisticated trench system with interconnecting saps enabling defenders to move between trenches, [and] fall back or reinforce a position in secrecy." In front of the trenches one found "a mass of concertina wire and acres of minefields," whereas further back, "every house, farm and building concealed 88mm guns, anti-tank guns, machine-guns and infantry." Still further back, "along the low, wooded hills the Germans had heavy guns ready to bombard a beachhead."[214]

Our DZ was an "egg-shaped" area, approximately 2000 yards east-west by 1500 yards north-south. The Field Orders for Operation Varsity describe the terrain and "obstructions" of our DZ as follows: "the main road which traverses the Zone from SW to NE roughly separates the Zone into two halves. The Southern half is very definitely 'bottom' land with a checkerboard pattern of shallow drainage ditches. Field boundaries are also generally separated by wire fences and occasionally a low hedge row. There are no farm yards or buildings in the bottom-land half of the Zone. A small stream (average width of water approximately 10') with the North bank slightly embanked, flows through the Zone approximately 100 yards South of the main road. There are a few trees (maximum height 30') intermittently along this stream. The Northern half of the Zone is also flat and level but is of slightly higher elevation than the bottom land. Field patterns are small and rectangular in shape. Field boundaries are free of trees, hedge rows, and ditches and apparently only the boundaries of farmsteads are separated by fences. Farm yards are largely confined to [the] North side of the main road

---

[214] Allen, <u>One More River</u>, p. 208. For another account of late-WWII movements across the Rhine, see William B. Breuer, <u>Storming Hitler's Rhine – The Allied Assault February – March 1945</u> (New York: St. Martins, 1985).

and near the wooded areas on the NW and East boundaries. Nearly all of the farm yards have adjacent orchards. Maximum height of farm buildings and surrounding trees is rarely in excess of 40′."

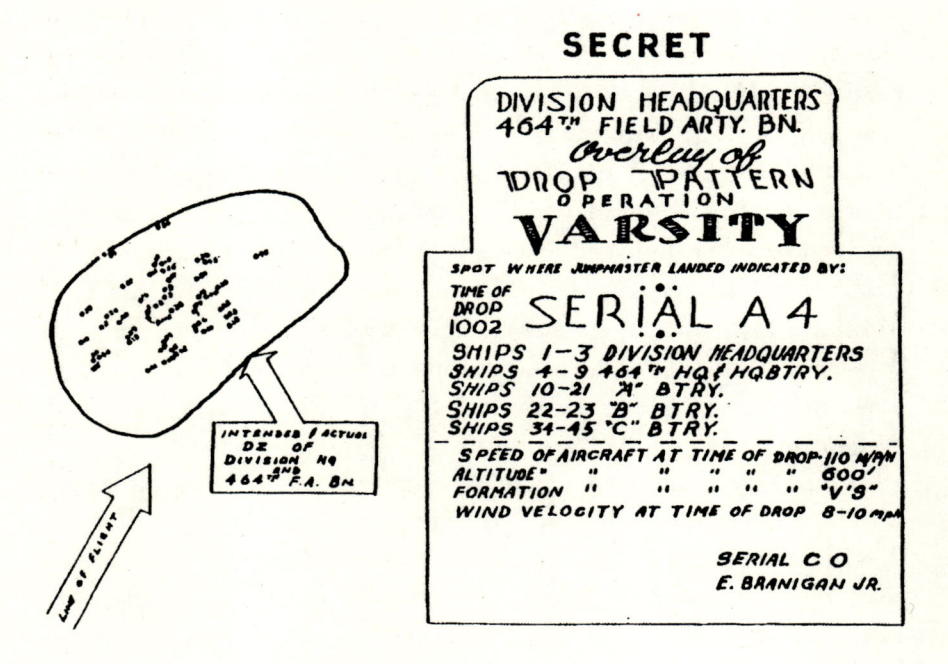

SECRET

Intended 464ᵗʰ Drop Pattern within DZ W

The "main SW-NE road is slightly embanked but is completely free of trees. Telephone and power lines line both sides of this road (pole height approximately 25′). A secondary road extending NW-SE through the bottom land near the Southwestern boundary of the area is embanked to a height of 10′ or better. A power line with poles approximately 25′ high runs along the Eastern side of this road. Another secondary road with an adjacent single track narrow gauge rail line runs along the woods on the North and NE boundaries of the Zone. It also has telephone and power line poles 25′-35′ high on both sides of [the] road. Minor roads in this Zone are level with the adjacent fields and free of trees. A small power line with poles approximately 10′ high follows the first minor road just North of and parallel to the main road. A concentration of bomb craters is present in the SW corner of the Zone. A small pond roughly 40′ in diameter is located [within the DZ]. Foxholes and occasional gun positions line both sides of the main road. The majority of farm yards and orchards have dug-in positions. Other defense gun positions, communication trenches, etc., form obstructions in this Zone."[215]

Wesel, the center of a major German communication network with some 24,600 people, served as a hub of water barge, road, and rail travel. Like Bastogne, Wesel was a critical crossroads area. It also served as the "principle artery" for shipping steel and coal from the Ruhr industrial region throughout Germany.[216] Curiously, as William Mitchell noted, Montgomery had previously considered invading Wesel instead of Arnhem in early September 1944. However, he was persuaded not to jump into Wesel back at that time "because of the thick antiflak defenses over the Ruhr." Six months later, Mitchell concluded, "the flak was still in place."[217]

The predominance of Roman Catholics in the Rhineland including Wesel had, at one time, established a "strong spiritual bloc to . . . German ideology." However, the "long years of political indoctrination, especially among the youth, has had the effect of lessening opposition to National Socialism."[218] Considering the recent "tremendous defeats" that the Germans had suffered in Russia and Africa and now in the west, coupled with "the hunger and privation due to the heavy Allied bombings of the past three years," the people continuing to populate the Rhineland had "lost much of their desire to continue the struggle."[219]

---

[215] "Field Order No. 5 for Operation Varsity," Annex No.1., p. 6.

[216] Ross, <u>Sky Men</u>, p. 272.

[217] William Mitchell, "Epilogue. One Last Great Jump," p. 255.

[218] Miley, "Varsity, Background Information," March 10, 1945., Annex 1a to Field Order No. 1., sheet 2 of 3. USAMHI.

[219] Miley, "Varsity, Background Information," March 10, 1945., Annex 1a to Field Order No. 1., sheet 3 of 3. USAMHI.

German Civilians Working for Allied Forces West of the Rhine Watching the Varsity Jump

We succeeded in accomplishing our aims in a matter of hours rather than days. Indeed, after a few hours, the enemy firing had slowed down considerably. The resistance was being cut down. Still, they were also achieving many of their targets as Allied planes were on fire and crashed around us for seemingly many hours. By nightfall, the enemy firing was diminished even more, suggesting that we had nearly achieved our aims.

Whenever we had the opportunity, we dug a foxhole. I had no idea how many hours or days I would be in any given spot, so I wanted to dig a deep foxhole. The thing about foxholes, however, is that you can never dig it deep enough – or fast enough. Every moment digging was a moment not firing my weapons, therefore, speed was of essence. One's trenching tool was as essential for survival on the battlefield as one's rifle.

You want to dig down so that you are level with the ground in order to feel somewhat protected, safe, and secure tucked beneath the ground level. If you could dig it deep enough to stand in or so that you also had to build some earthen steps to get out, all the better. I never knew who might be dropping in, especially those who, for whatever reasons, had no time to dig a foxhole of their own. Bomb craters made a great start for foxholes, as long as they were not too close to any water. Not knowing how long I would be in any position, I wanted to be sure to keep the water out my foxhole.

The mission of Operation Varsity was "to seize, clear and secure the Division area with priority to the high ground east of Diersfordt . . . and the bridges over the Issel River, [to] protect the right (South) flank of Corps; [and to] establish contact with the 1st Commando Brigade, the 12th British Corps and the 6th British Airborne Division."[220]All of these efforts would further "assist the Allied breakout once the Rhine barrier was breached."[221] Capturing (or "bouncing") the bridges would also prevent any possible influx of German reinforcements.

Bomb Craters around a Destroyed Wesel

---

[220] "Historical Report of Operation Varsity," p. 1.
[221] Thompson, U.S. Airborne in Action, p.34.

Initially, we had been firing in one direction, and for hours we held our position without advancing forward. We continued to fire, though at times we could not see our specific targets. Thus, we were less dependent upon being able to recognize the enemy than were our brothers in the infantry. Rather, we in the 464th artillery had a forward observer, who gained information by radio about the positions of our enemy and communicated it back to us. We then set the elevation of our howitzers and adjusted the amount of powder needed to cover the distance of our shells. Bomb craters covered the ground, and it would not have been possible to advance with any ease in certain directions. During the early part of the following day's battle, we were directed to turn our howitzer 180 degrees and resume firing toward this newly established target area.[222]

Parachutes Over Wesel, March 24, 1945

[222] Don R. Pay, "Operational Diary 17th Airborne Division Covering January 1, 1945 to April 10, 1945," (St. Paul, MN: Mel Therrien, 1993), p. 24. Page numbering reflects the hand numbering system in Mel Therrien's copy in the USAMHI archives. Therrien was historian of the 17th Airborne Division Association.

After an hour or so of fighting after my jump, I began to notice that many of our planes were still flying over, dropping troops and gliders around the forest. Parachutes also covered the ground and were hanging on nearly every remaining high structure.[223] As one writer later quipped, there was "enough silk to start a riot at Macy's."[224] Although I kept my attention on my mission, I could not help noticing that the sky was full of paratroopers and gliders. Like most troopers in the 17th, we jumped into combat with green nylon 28-foot-diameter camouflage chutes. We were later given a scarf made from, so we were told, chutes recovered from the ground that day. As any additional protection from the enemy was helpful, camouflage was definitely a good choice especially for the first of the serials to jump. Colorful chutes (or parapacks) of blue, red and yellow were also flowing down, color-coded according to the types of supply bundles and equipment containers that they were carrying. Even Jeeps and anti-tank guns were dropping from Short Stirling bombers in paired or clustered chutes, each 32-feet in diameter.[225] The gliderists followed the paratroopers in hopes that the troopers would assemble their weapons and diminish some of the German defense before the majority of the gliders had landed.[226] To reinforce our fire power, the 83rd Light Regiment of Britain's Royal Army provided general arms support from the west bank of the Rhine.[227]

Unbeknownst to me, and to nearly all of the troopers that day, we were "on parade" during this jump. Montgomery, who had arranged every elaborate detail of this airborne assault, had gathered Eisenhower

---

[223] Despite the best efforts of the 17th Airborne Parachute Maintenance Company beginning on our D-Day, only a "small amount of this equipment either undamaged or damaged was eventually recovered." "Historical Report of Operation Varsity," p. 15.

[224] Frank Langston and Justin P. Buckridge (eds), The Talon Crosses the Rhine (Paris: E. Desfossés-Néogravure, 1945), "D-Day at Wesel" section, photo caption.

[225] Gregory, United States Airborne Forces, p. 37.

[226] For an account of the gliderists who participated in Varsity from the Royal Air Force perspective, see Alan Cooper, Wot? No Engines!: RAF Glider Pilots and Operation Varsity (Bognor Regis, U.K.: Woodfield Publishing, 2002).

[227] "Historical Report of Operation Varsity," p. 17.

and Churchill with him, together with Generals Brereton and Ridgway, on the western bank of the Rhine. Eisenhower claimed that he was "struck by the courage of the transport pilots flying relatively slow aircraft steadily along their allotted routes in spite of heavy flak damage."[228] Churchill was also moved with courage and optimism by this panoramic view. "My dear General," he stated to Eisenhower while watching the Varsity drop from their west bank post, "The German is whipped. We've got him. He is all through."[229]

Churchill, Eisenhower, and Montgomery Observing the Rhine Jump, March 24, 1945

Two hours after the initial troopers had landed, 240 U.S. 8th Air Force B-24 Liberators flew overhead on the tail of the last troop carriers

---

[228] "Supreme Commanders Dispatch for Operations in Northwest Europe," p. 96.
[229] Garrett, "Airborne through the Ages," p. 63.

in a deafening thunder cloud dropping 580 tons of needed supplies.[230] Nearly all of these supplies were recovered, with little going into enemy hands. Our battalion benefited greatly from these Liberators' ammunition resupply. Everything in the sky looked relatively close from a ground perspective. As far as you could see, nothing overhead in the sky seemed more than a thousand feet away. Planes descended and ascended all around us, some crashing, having been hit by enemy fire. Twenty-two of the planes that went down in flames that day were the C-46 "flying coffins." Fortunately, the jumpers in "all but one" managed to get out, although the crews in many of the other crashed planes did not survive.[231] Overall 44 transport aircraft and 80 gliders were destroyed by anti-aircraft fire on Operation Varsity's D-Day.[232] The losses during the first two hours alone were the highest ever sustained in airborne warfare.[233]

Planes continued to fly all around us from above. The majority of the other DZs and LZs were along the eastern and northern edges of the forest. Montgomery's smoke screen effectively blanketed much of the area, thereby preventing many pilots and navigators from identifying precise DZs. Pilots had been ordered to release troopers and gliders "as near to the assault area as possible" on their "first pass" even if they failed to locate their designated DZs or LZs.[234]

---

[230] Mitchell, "Epilogue. One Last Great Jump," p. 266, and Bilstein, Airlift and Airborne Operations in World War II, p. 37. Fifteen of these aircraft were shot down and another 104 damaged by enemy fire after they had dropped their supplies. USAF Airborne Operations, p. 89.

[231] Gregory, United States Airborne Forces, p. 122, and Mitchell, "One Last Great Jump," p. 263.

[232] Gregory, United States Airborne Forces, pp. 122-123.

[233] Mitchell, "One Last Great Jump," p. 263.

[234] "Field Order No. 5 for Operation Varsity," p. 6.

U.S. Troopers and Gliders in German Soil, March 24, 1945

The parachute drops of Col. Raff's 507th Combat Team were estimated to be 67% successful in terms of landing in their DZs. Raff's own serial landed "more than two miles northwest of DZ "W," near Diersfordter Castle." The next serial dropped only a mile northwest of their target. Gen. Miley together with Branigan's 464th landed much more on target within DZ "W."[235] James Stock claimed that this pattern illustrated the "mixed fortunes" typical of airborne drops. "Most battles are confused and . . . chaotic affairs," he acknowledged, but "a battle fought by airborne soldiers, spread over a wide area, is doubly so."[236] Fortunately, the scattered men of the 507th rejoined the rest of their regiment within a relatively short time. Most battalions were, in due course, able to assemble much more quickly on the ground than they had in previous airborne operations. In effect, the Allied forces had surrounded much of the forest, and the Germans were forced to fight hard just to hold their own lines.

---

[235] C. Blair, <u>Ridgway's Paratroopers</u>, p. 457.
[236] J. Stock, <u>Rhine Crossing</u>, p. 134.

"Am I mistaken, or did I hear one of you give a long, low whistle?"

The action of the 464th "pummeling the woodlands" with their howitzers "made it plain that DZ "W" was going to stay in *Amerikaner* hands."[237] German troops that had initially been stationed along the eastern side of the Rhine to counter allied attempts to cross the river later entered into the fray as they moved in to support their forces within the forest. The artillery component of Raff's Combat Team showed "equal élan" to his infantry.[238]

Dead and wounded soldiers were scattered across our field, though you could walk a hundred yards at times without encountering another dead soldier. The medics, who had jumped with us and who were being yelled for throughout the day, attended to the wounded as soon as they could reach them. It is very hard to see a brother lying dead, but war is war, and we managed to trudge along.

Later in the day, medics crossed the field in larger numbers in attempt to retrieve the dead and severely wounded troopers. Ambulance transport across the Rhine had been delayed, and they did not reach

---

[237] Andrews, <u>Airborne Album</u>, p. 76.
[238] Hickey, <u>Out of the Sky</u>, p. 181.

the battlefield until the next day.[239] Some of the Germans who had been captured were put to work "as litter bearers," and were forced to "dig foxholes and litter trenches for patients."[240] German medics who had been captured were "given medical supplies and employed to treat their own wounded."[241] They, like we, saw lots of German bodies that were swollen and bloated, who had probably been killed in the previous days' strafing of the area.

The stench of this battle was, at times, overpowering. Fortunately, we moved along the ground a great deal, usually advancing further ahead. Thus, the stench that we encountered at one moment soon left our senses as we moved passed it. We also concentrated our efforts to remove the battlefield carnage that we witnessed from our minds as well as we could.

We encountered heavy firing throughout our D-Day, but it was not as prolonged as it had been in other battles. Still, according to one U.S. officer, the intensity of the incoming fire was much greater than he had experienced at Normandy. A British officer claimed the German's heavy defensive firing made "Arnhem look like a Sunday picnic."[242] Captain Eric Friedheim agreed, arguing that the ground opposition he faced in Varsity was "much more intense than [that] in Normandy and Holland." Such intensity, he claimed, was due to the "limited area involved in the landings."[243]

The enemy appeared to still have a number of active tanks, and we had known throughout the war that the German artillery was top notch. I'll admit that the Germans were, and had been, good fighters. The Nazis had conditioned them through their militaristic upbringing. This nurturing had been forced upon them, and they had much more knowledge of the military as kids than we had received. Back towards the beginning of the war, the German soldiers in their prime were highly trained, armed, and knowledgeable. At that time, their weaponry may well have been superior to ours. Such well conditioned

---

[239] "Historical Report of Operation Varsity," p. 27.
[240] "Historical Report of Operation Varsity," p. 27.
[241] "Historical Report of Operation Varsity," p. 27.
[242] Mitchell, "Epilogue. One Last Great Jump," p. 263.
[243] Friedheim, "Rhineland Rendezvous," p. 58.

German soldiers were not, however, what we primarily encountered in March 1945.

Throughout the day, individual soldiers or groups of Germans surrendered. By 1800 hours, the "Stars & Stripes" was flying over Diersfordter Castle.[244] We had been told to "Take no prisoners" as we landed, but rather, to shoot them and plow forward, focused upon our mission. These orders were likely carried out all around the forest during the early hours of the battle. However, as the day proceeded, the number

---

[244] Barrie Quarrie, <u>Airborne Assault: Parachute Forces in Action, 1940-1991</u> (Somerset, United Kingdom: Patrick Stevens, Ltd., 1991), p. 138.

of German soldiers who surrendered was escalating. The 464th used some of these captured Germans to help tow their cannons.[245] Many of these prisoners appeared quite haggard. They were tired, older men who must have been fighting for many months. They acted as though the end of the war was near, and they had deemed to give up than fight. In the Bulge, U.S. forces had learned not to shoot surrendering Germans, for other Germans who saw their comrades killed upon surrender were more likely to hold strong in their positions.[246] Although you still had to watch out for the occasional sons of a gun who falsely waived white flags, the enemy at this time was not as fierce as they had been a few years earlier. It was easier to sympathize with them as tired soldiers than as they had appeared in the propaganda through which we had originally come to know our enemy. People on this earth are all God's people. Still, the Germans were the enemy, and I questioned why they had done what they did to start this war in Europe.

To meet the large number of prisoners that were accumulating, special areas were designated by the end of the first day of battle to secure and care for them. Early the next day, one Allied official who "had established three small prisoner of war enclosures" close to the Rhine, each of which accommodated 50 prisoners, was notified that "he had two hours in which to provide accommodations for 3500 German prisoners."[247]

As night fell following the day of our jump, we remained with our howitzers, ready for action wherever needed. We had a sufficient re-supply of ammunition to meet forces that we might encounter. We had our code words as well. "Thunder" had been our code for encounters with an unknown individual before 1200 hours on D-Day, and "Hither" was used for any encounters thereafter.[248] Guns continued to fire throughout the night, lighting the sky like fireworks. Hinson of the 464th recalls that "the whole sky was lighted" with tracer fire. "I had no idea where it was coming from or where it was going to land," he noted.[249] Overall, the whole situation was eerie and frightening. In

---

[245] Wade C. Hinson to Robert L. Wilson, December 13, 2003.
[246] Ross also made this point in Sky Men, p. 282.
[247] "Narrative of Operation Varsity," p. 11.
[248] Friedheim, "Rhineland Rendezvous," p. 28.
[249] Wade C. Hinson to Robert L. Wilson, December 13, 2003.

contrast to the loud air fire overhead, our position remained relatively quiet. We had our rations to eat, and we had dug our foxholes and slit trenches nearby for latrine needs. Some caught a quick nap as they could, while others remained alert. It was hard to think of sleeping with everything that was going on around and above us even though we had already experienced a stress-filled and eventful day.

Having given my personal account, I would like to turn to an "Official History" of the day's action, specifically in regard to the 464th PFAB in order to provide a more objective perspective. Upon landing in their DZ, the 464th "immediately came under small arms fire from areas adjacent to the DZ. This battalion set up three 50 caliber machine guns on the DZ and fired into the woods in attempt to neutralize the enemy fire."[250] The enemy was some "200 yards away."[251] Within "a few minutes of the drop, three howitzers were set up on the DZ and commenced direct fire on enemy emplacements in the vicinity. The artillery fires in the DZ were a large factor in neutralizing the enemy fires and demoralizing their forces. By 1200, the battalion had four howitzers operating in the previously selected positions approximately 1500 yards NE of the DZ. Twelve field pieces had been dropped by the battalion. By 1300, nine of these were in action in the previously selected positions, three were damaged and parts were salvaged from these to assemble the tenth howitzer shortly after 1300."[252] Although the men in one battalion had landed well within our DZ, some of our equipment was dropped in the trees 1500 yards to the northwest of our DZ, and thus we "had to fight as infantry to recover it."[253]

We could tell little of the overall picture from our gun positions, but it was later reported that the Division's mission had been "accomplished in every particular within a few hours after landing. It was accomplished in the face of heavy flak and heavy initial resistance on and around the landing areas by enemy troops who had been ordered to sleep at their gun positions the preceding night."[254]

---

[250] "Historical Report of Operation Varsity," p. 2.
[251] Crookenden, Airborne at War, p. 128.
[252] "Historical Report of Operation Varsity," p. 2.
[253] Samuel C. Myer, "Varsity's Organic Artillery," Field Artillery Journal, 35 (1945): 637.
[254] "Historical Report of Operation Varsity," p. 6.

Although it was much later before I had any indication of our battalion's specific achievements of that day, we eventually learned that we 400 men in Branigan's Bastard Battalion, were the "first Airborne Field Artillery Unit, either parachute or glider, to land, fight, and fire its guns East of the Rhine River. This Battalion, together with men of Raff's 507th, took the brunt of the initial fighting." Raff, himself, had jumped first in his stick from the lead plane.[255] The "relatively few casualties" of these units, as later recorded, was attributed "to better training and leadership, not to lighter enemy action."[256] In General Miley's later citation accompanying Branigan's award of the Bonze Star Medal, Miley noted that "So thoroughly were his men trained and so well were they briefed on their participation in the operation that their mission was accomplished with unqualified success."[257]

All of the farm houses in the surrounding area had been rifled or shelled. We used them as artillery targets assuming that enemy snipers or saboteurs may be hiding within. A few days after landing, one trooper and I went to scout out a partially bombed farm house. With our loaded rifles poised, we searched what remained of the ground floor of this house then proceeded to the basement. We found no one "at home." We did, however, find a large trunk in the basement. We examined it for wires and booby traps as best we could. Finding none, we decided to open it and plunder. In order to each use both of our hands to delve into the unknown treasures, we leaned our rifles against another piece of furniture nearby. As we were going through the trunk, we both heard something move behind us – something between us and the basement steps. We realized that we were just out of arm's reach from our rifles. We looked sharply at each other, quickly signaled, then lunged for our rifles and rolled around ready to shoot – only to find a dog that had come out of hiding. The dog seemed very happy to see us, but he was nowhere near as happy as we were to learn that the noise we had heard had come only from a dog. We played with that

---

[255] Flanagan, <u>Airborne: A Combat History</u>, p. 292.

[256] Branigan's comments. According to the "Historical Report of Operation Varsity," p.8, the total battle casualties for the 17th Division for Operation Varsity, as reported at 2400, March 25, 1945, totaled 1307, of which 393 were men killed in action, 834 were men wounded in action, and 80 men missing in action.

[257] Miley Citation.

dog quite a bit before moving on. I learned several lasting lessons from that "scouting expedition." After then, I never laid my rifle down when exploring any structure – nor did I pursue any further plundering.[258]

Although most of the farm houses had been attacked, a few remained in which civilians who were "not suspected of aiding the enemy or offering armed resistance" were secured for twenty-four hours. After that time, "one female person from each household" was permitted to leave the house briefly "for the purpose of feeding livestock and obtaining food and water," but she was "not permitted to use roads."[259]

Some attention must be directed to those fighters who, for two days prior to our jump, had heavily bombed the region from the skies. Air attacks were directed against nearby communication centers, military installations and airfields. 8,508 U.S. tons of bombs had been dropped on railroad centers and road junctions, destroying at least 80 locomotives and 2,383 railroad cars. Much of Wesel and the buildings in the surrounding countryside, together with military barracks had been leveled. Some partial buildings remained standing, and many of them had Germans inside. They had to be taken. Ten airfields had been destroyed as had numerous enemy aircraft both in flight and on the ground.[260] Curiously, another strategic air mission was occurring elsewhere in Germany simultaneous to our Airborne invasion. The 15th Air Force with 150 heavy bombers flew "one of its longest missions," to bomb Berlin, in part, to "draw enemy fighters to the east away from the invasion area."[261]

---

[258] On March 27, General Miley argued that despite "previous orders forbidding looting . . . personnel of this command are ransacking, pillaging and looting homes and leaving them in a deplorable condition." Such action was to "cease immediately," he ordered. Major General Miley "Memorandum," March 27, 1945., in George L. Streuker's Papers, Box 1, "After Action Report Maps, 17th Airborne Division, 1945" folder, USAMHI.

[259] Major General Miley "Memorandum," March 27, 1945., in George L. Streuker's Papers, Box 1, "After Action Report Maps, 17th Airborne Division, 1945" Folder, USAMHI.

[260] "Report of the Allied Air Operations in Preparation for, and in Connection with, Operations 'Plunder' and 'Varsity,'" March 28, 1945, pp. 4-5.

[261] "Narrative of Operation Varsity," p. 8.

As Bart Hagerman rightly reminds us, the airborne assault "could not have taken place" without the previous efforts of the Division Land Echelon. A 2,005 vehicle convoy was involved in a 24-hour drive covering 246 miles over two land routes. Their mission was to have all the heavy equipment as well as additional food, ammunition, and medical supplies across the river to meet the needs of the airborne assault teams. They met this mission and continued their drive unimpeded to their assembly sites near Issum and Kapellen on the western banks of the Rhine.[262] The careful tactical planning and efficient coordination of this overland movement was, indeed, a critical factor in the overall success of the Rhine crossings.

In summarizing Germany's response to Operation Varsity, Breuer described that "In his deep bunker under the garden of the Reich Chancellery in pulverized Berlin," Adolf Hitler "flew into a rage" over the news that Montgomery's 21st Army Group was over the Rhine in strength. The *Führer* "promptly ordered poison gas [to] be unleashed against the Wesel and other Allied bridgeheads east of the Rhine" and that "thousands of American and British airmen who were POWs in the Third Reich" be shot. "Cooler heads, pointing out that the Allies could retaliate in a far more massive scale, prevailed."[263]

---

[262] Hagerman, "Operation Varsity," p. 137.
[263] Breuer, Geronimo, p. 559.

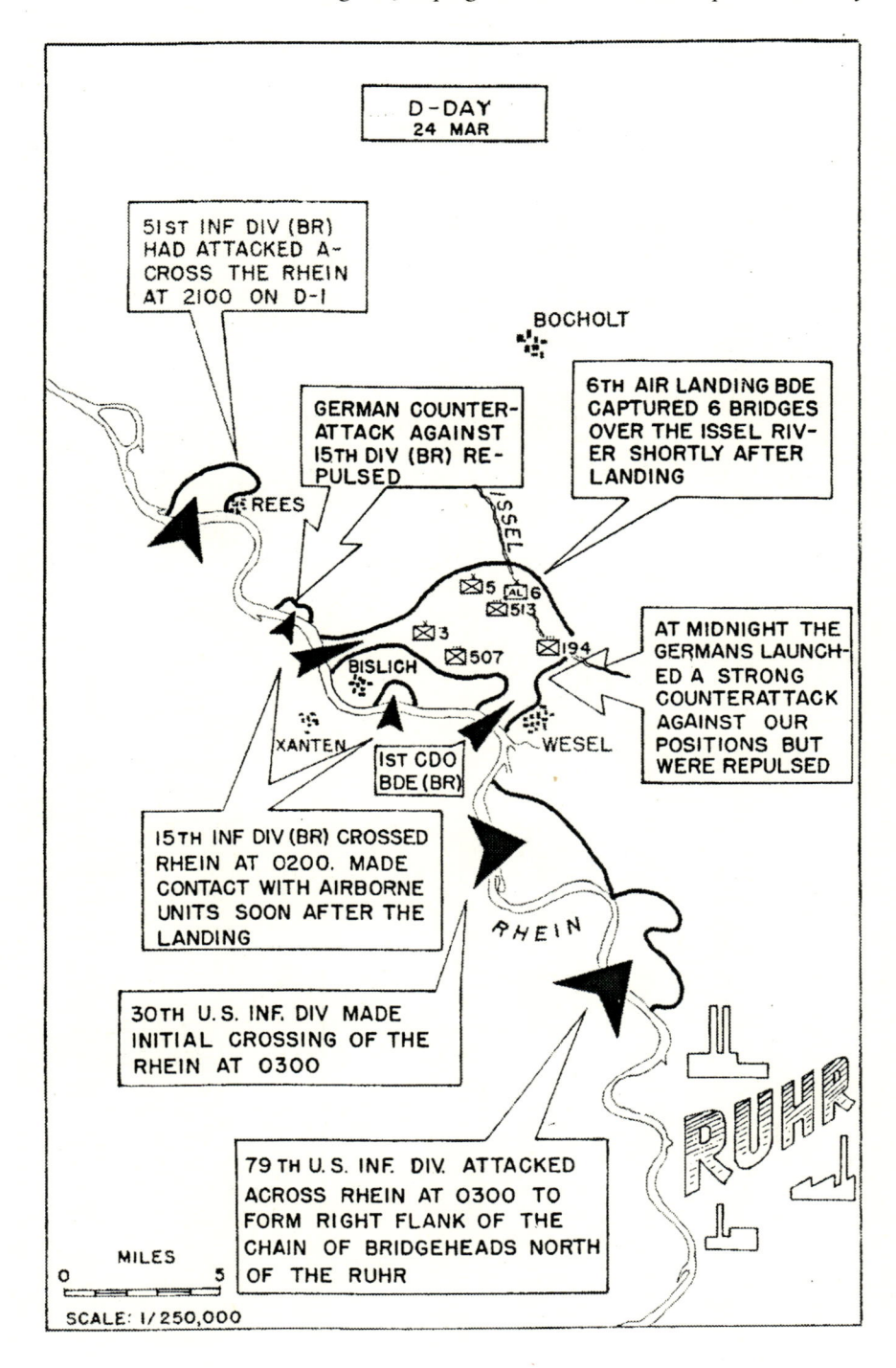

D-DAY
24 MAR

51ST INF DIV (BR) HAD ATTACKED A-CROSS THE RHEIN AT 2100 ON D-1

BOCHOLT

GERMAN COUNTER-ATTACK AGAINST 15TH DIV (BR) RE-PULSED

6TH AIR LANDING BDE CAPTURED 6 BRIDGES OVER THE ISSEL RIV-ER SHORTLY AFTER LANDING

REES

ISSEL

5 AL 6
513
3
507 194

AT MIDNIGHT THE GERMANS LAUNCH-ED A STRONG COUNTERATTACK AGAINST OUR POSITIONS BUT WERE REPULSED

BISLICH

XANTEN

1ST CDO BDE (BR)

WESEL

15TH INF DIV (BR) CROSSED RHEIN AT 0200. MADE CONTACT WITH AIRBORNE UNITS SOON AFTER THE LANDING

RHEIN

30TH U.S. INF. DIV MADE INITIAL CROSSING OF THE RHEIN AT 0300

RUHR

MILES
0   5

79TH U.S. INF. DIV. ATTACKED ACROSS RHEIN AT 0300 TO FORM RIGHT FLANK OF THE CHAIN OF BRIDGEHEADS NORTH OF THE RUHR

SCALE: 1/250,000

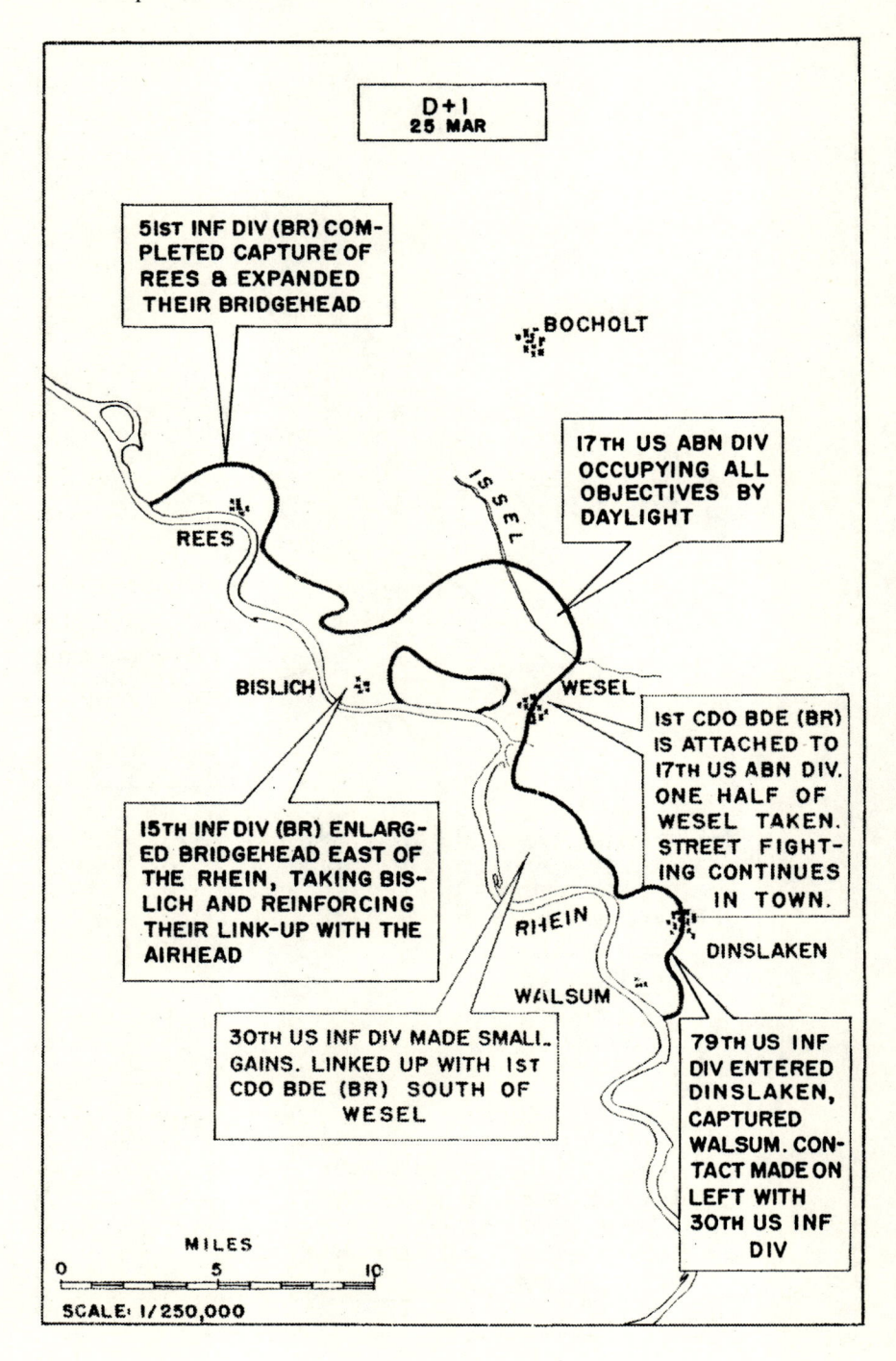

The following day (D+1) is much less clear in my mind. We remained on the battlefield, and after time, we moved a bit further east towards Munster. Fortunately, Captain Don R. Pay, the public relations officer of the 17th Division, recorded the activities of the 507th Combat Team, including our battalion.[264] On Sunday, March 25, the 507th "completed the clearing of the area . . . during the early morning hours . . . and prepared to launch an attack." "Light resistance was encountered but it was not in sufficient strength to appreciabl[y] delay the advance. Temporary defensive positions were established for the night."[265] A series of "phase lines" to the east of Wesel were designed in order to coordinate the allied advance. We in the 507th CT were organized along phase line London.[266]

We moved our guns in harnesses as needed. Although these howitzer shells were, at 3 inches in diameter, only an inch less than the diameter of the shells of the 105 howitzers we trained on at Camp Mackall, the whole gun was considerably lighter and easier to maneuver. Other artillery pieces, including the new 57mm and 75 mm recoilless rifles had "their baptism of fire against German tanks" that day, and both were found to be great improvements over the bazookas.[267]

---

[264] Don R. Pay, "Operational Diary, 17th Airborne Division, covering January 1, 1945 to April 10, 1945.

[265] Pay, "Operational Diary," p. 24. The "Historical Report of Operation Varsity," p. 9, suggests that "After enemy forces were driven out of Wesel pocket and east of the Rhine direct contact was lost for a number of days, and during this period little accurate information on enemy intentions or dispositions was received."

[266] John Marr, "507th Parachute Infantry Regiment," in B. Hagerman (ed) U.S.A. Airborne 50th Anniversary, p. 275.

[267] Thomspon, U.S. Airborne in Action, p. 34.

Pfc. Wilson on Combat Field, Germany, March 1945

On the following day, the time during which the airborne phase of the operation was officially transferred to ground forces, the enemy "endeavored to build a semblance of a defensive line from Brunen to Drevenack." This defense "took the form of a series of small unit positions partially dug in, only slightly supported by artillery." Interrogation of some of the 3,246 prisoners captured since the beginning of the assault revealed that the remaining enemy troops in this sector were "greatly disorganized, lacking communications, and [lacking] heavy weapons support."[268]

---

[268] Pay, "Operational Diary," p. 24.

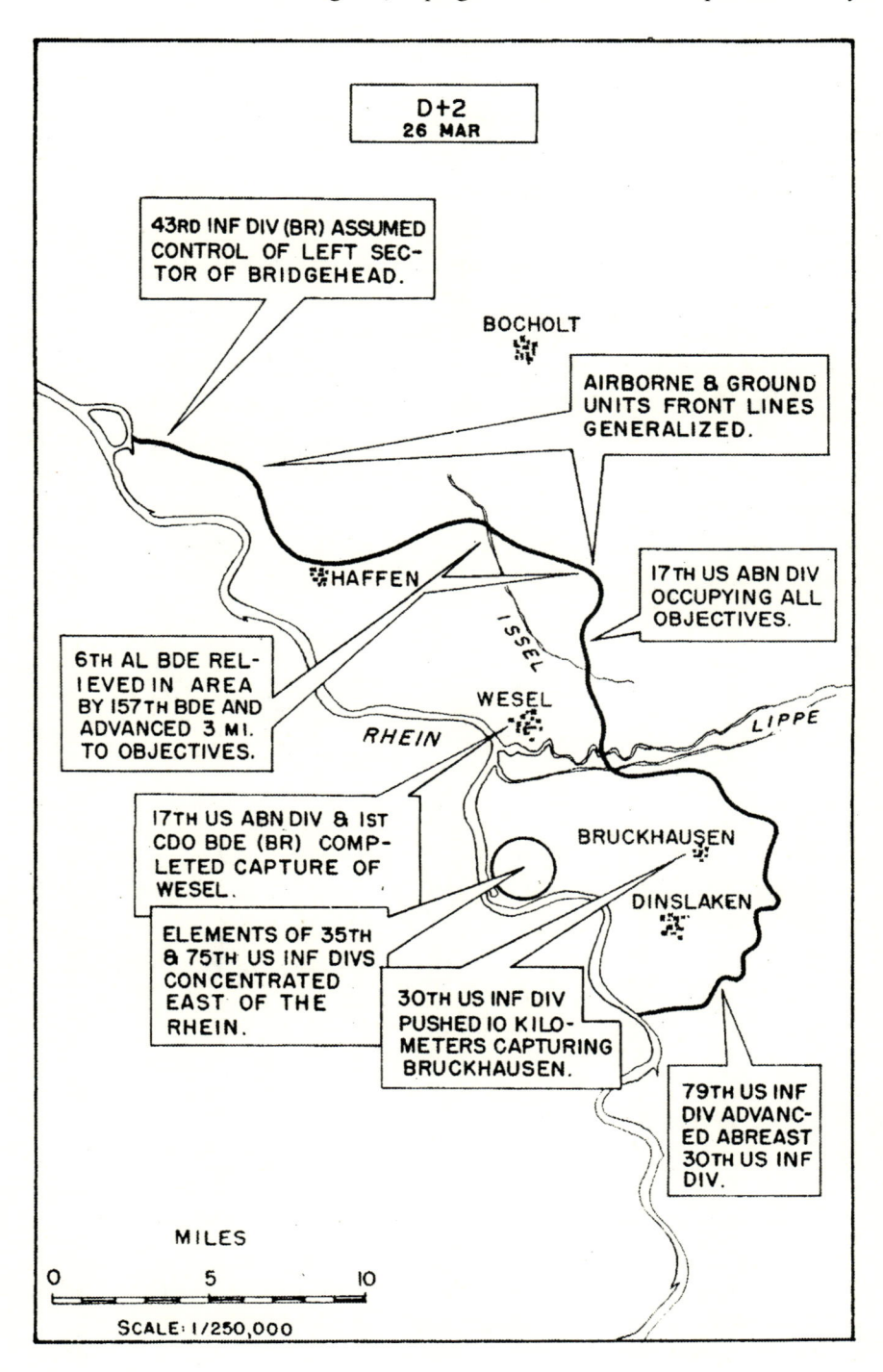

D+2
26 MAR

43RD INF DIV (BR) ASSUMED CONTROL OF LEFT SECTOR OF BRIDGEHEAD.

BOCHOLT

AIRBORNE & GROUND UNITS FRONT LINES GENERALIZED.

HAFFEN

ISSEL

17TH US ABN DIV OCCUPYING ALL OBJECTIVES.

6TH AL BDE RELIEVED IN AREA BY 157TH BDE AND ADVANCED 3 MI. TO OBJECTIVES.

WESEL

RHEIN

LIPPE

17TH US ABN DIV & 1ST CDO BDE (BR) COMPLETED CAPTURE OF WESEL.

BRUCKHAUSEN

ELEMENTS OF 35TH & 75TH US INF DIVS CONCENTRATED EAST OF THE RHEIN.

DINSLAKEN

30TH US INF DIV PUSHED 10 KILOMETERS CAPTURING BRUCKHAUSEN.

79TH US INF DIV ADVANCED ABREAST 30TH US INF DIV.

MILES

0   5   10

SCALE: 1/250,000

As part of the 11 kilometer advance on the following day, March 27, we in the 507th CT captured our objectives and "continued to attack east against increasing resistance." Encountering "intermittent artillery fire" and "continuous" "harassing fire" from the enemy on the next day, the 507th "accomplished its mission entirely, cleared [the] sector [of enemies] and captured the town of Wolten." This capture included 79 enlisted men and one officer, the destruction of 3 enemy SP's [self-propelled howitzers] and one enemy ammunition dump.[269] Front line elements of the 17th Division, including the 507th, advanced 28 kilometers, from Haltern to Dulmen, clearing the enemy on March 29 and organizing a "perimeter of defense of this area." At the close of that day, all battalions were "continuing to improve their positions and conducting extensive patrolling on all sides." It appears that "the enemy is withdrawing as rapidly as opportunity permits and [is] attempting to salvage units for a final stand, possibly on the Dortmund-EMS canal or the Weser River line."[270]

---

[269] Pay, "Operational Diary," pp. 25-26. For a chronicle of the 507th Parachute Infantry Regiment's actions during the days following the Rhine jump, see John Marr's "507th Parachute Infantry Regiment," esp. pp. 275-277.

[270] Pay, "Operational Diary," p. 27.

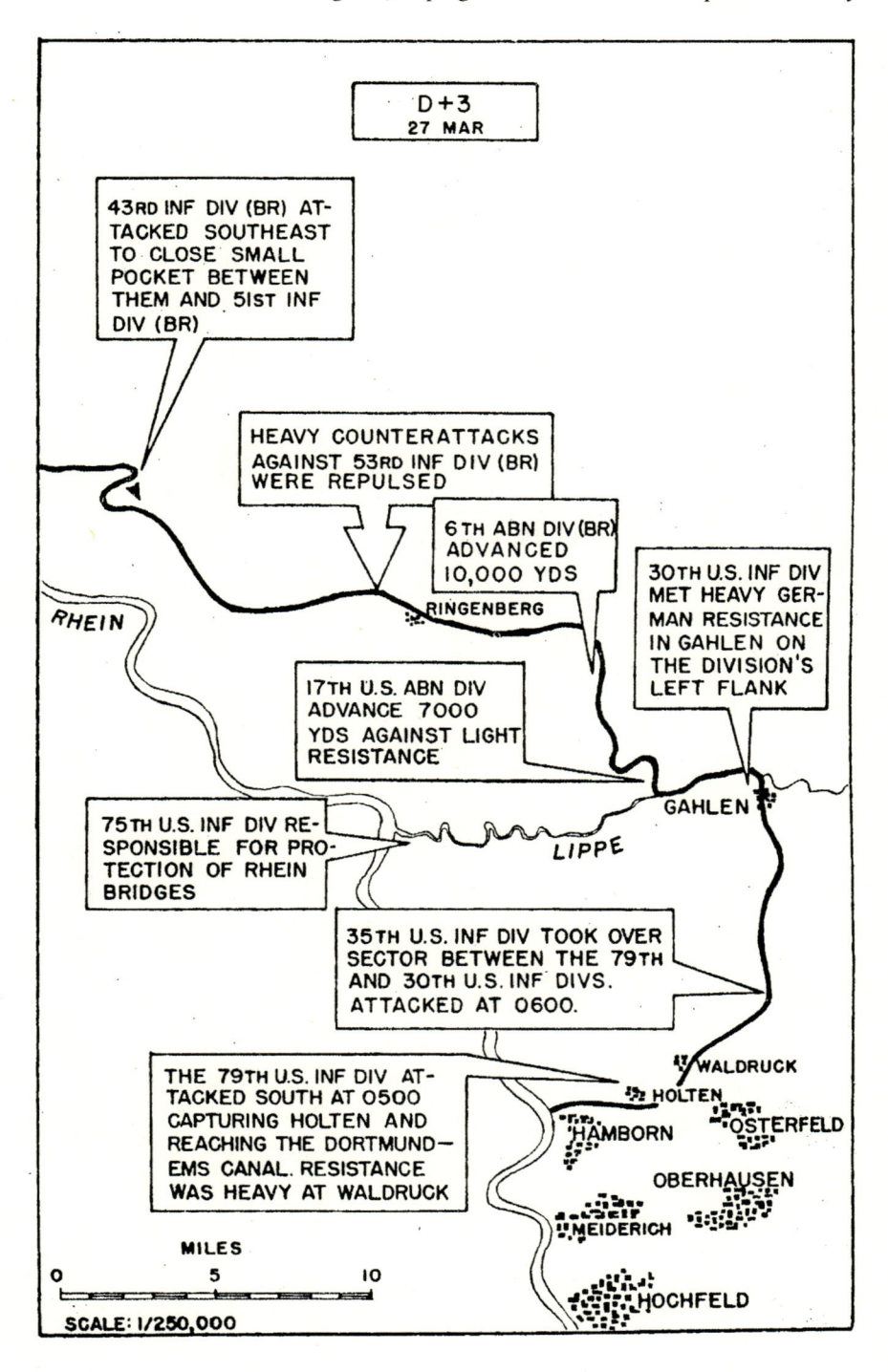

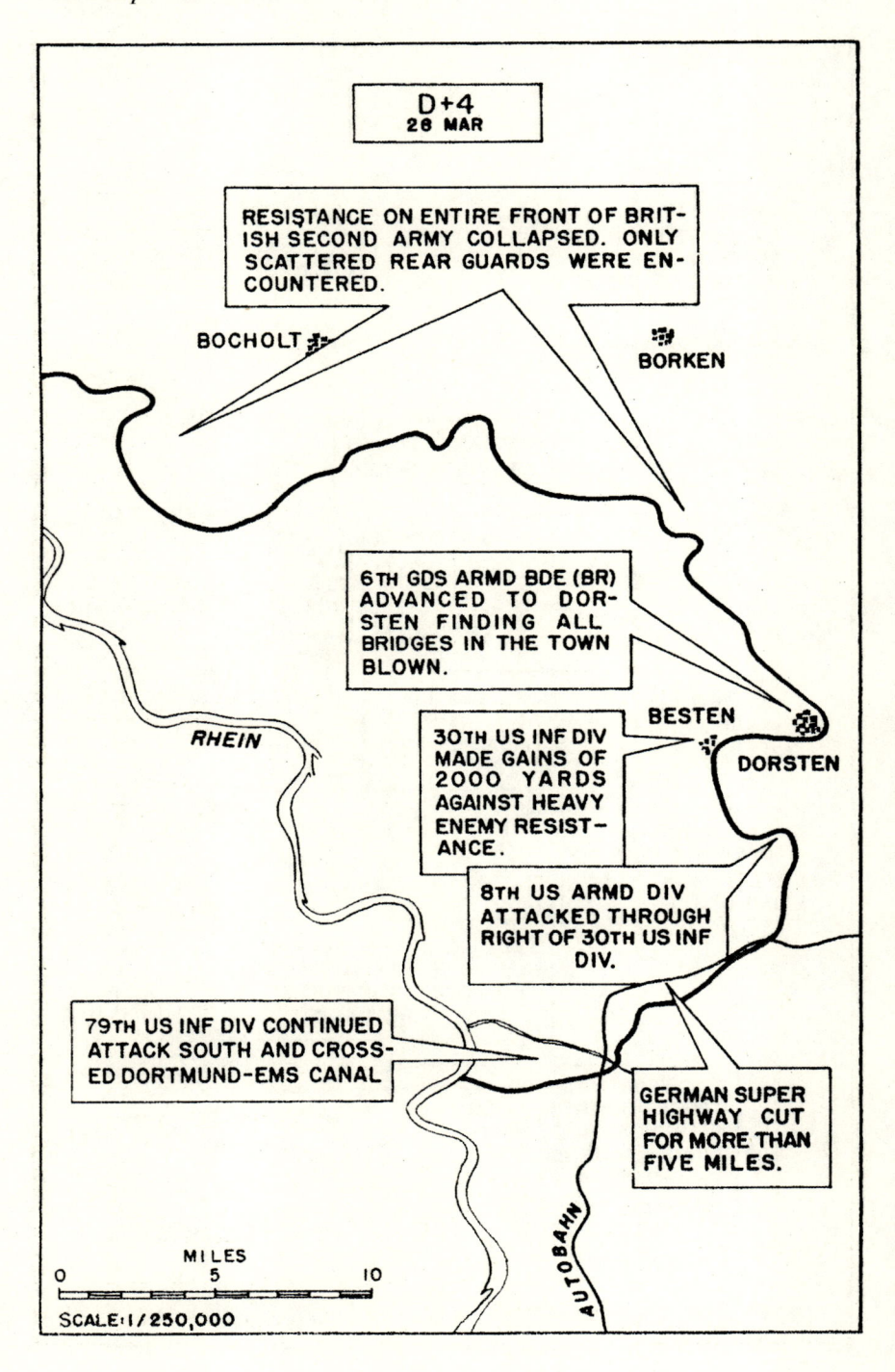

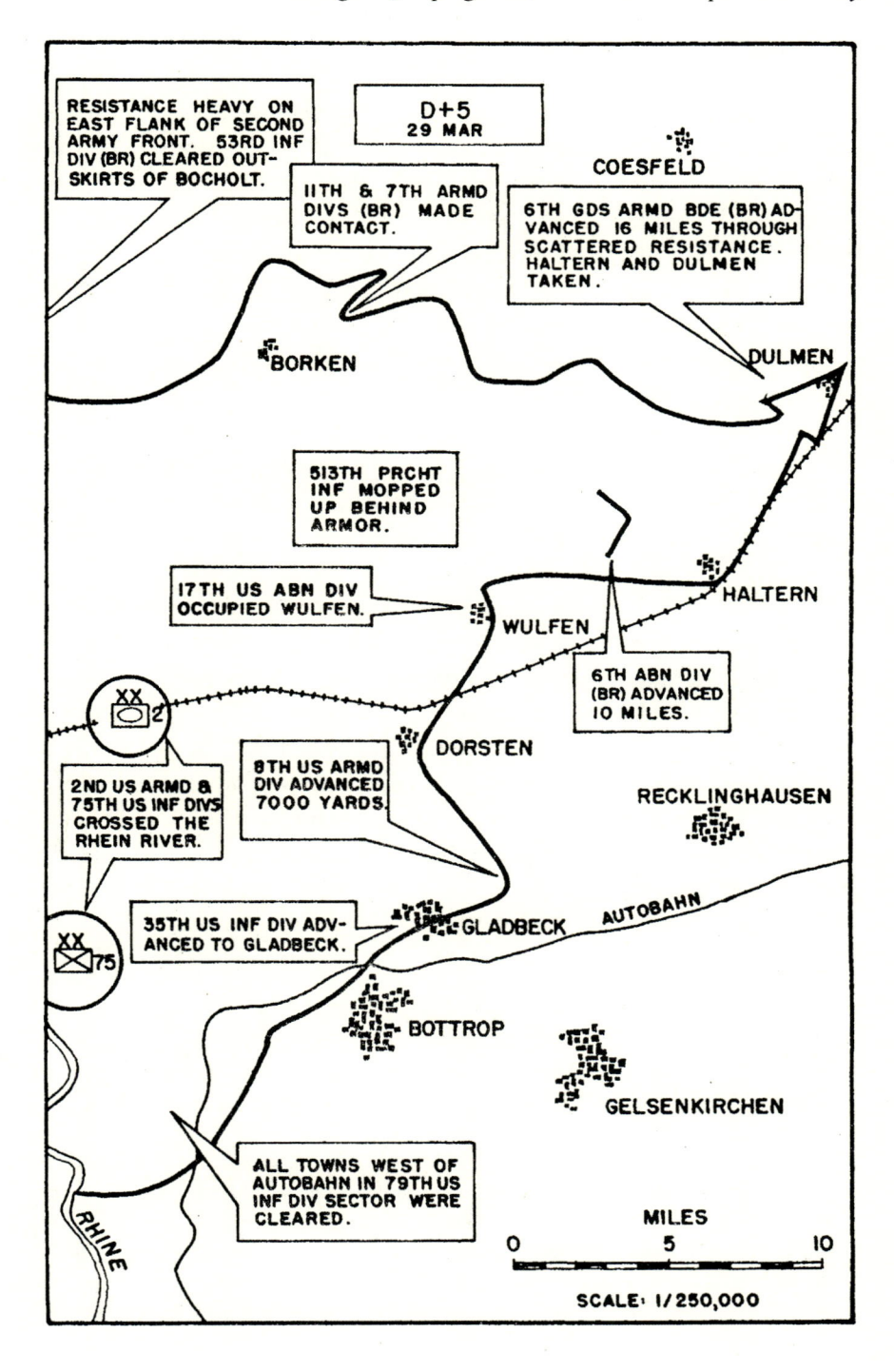

The Division held fast for several days. The 507th maintained "perimeter defense of Haltern and the area northeast of the town." In this capacity we remained "very active patrolling . . . the front of all positions." We faced a counterattack from the enemy at 1900 on March 31, fighting with a strength of "approximately one company supported by artillery" firing "from across the river to the south." This counterattack was "repelled . . . with heavy losses resulting for the enemy." The Divisional Regiments were reorganized this day, too, but the 507th remained under XIX Corps command.[271]

Within six days, the XVIII Corps (Airborne) had advanced a total of forty-one miles and captured 8,009 prisoners. General Ridgway acknowledged that this success was achieved "not by the remarkable circumstance of having events develop according to schedule, but rather by thousands of individuals who through bold and aggressive action, [and] by tireless and intelligent efforts caused those events to occur."[272]

The "American soldier is ingenious," according to Branigan, and the "paratroopers more so." In later recollections of the days following the jump, Branigan claimed that his men "found, liberated, and used wheelbarrows, farm carts, wagons, baby carriages, a Mercedes staff car with a shot up radiator that needed water every few hundred yards, two horses, one cow, and a few of our ammunition carts that had survived the drop. All these items were used to haul our wounded, the ammunition and equipment. We may have looked like 'Coxie's [sic] Army,' with the men hauling the guns by hand and brute power, but the fighting never stopped."[273]

---

[271] Pay, "Operational Diary," pp. 28-29.

[272] "Operation Varsity 23 March, 1945 to 30 March 1945," XVIII Corps (Airborne), p. 11. For other personal anecdotal accounts of Operation Varsity, see Bart Hagerman (ed) War Stories: The Men of the Airborne (Paducah, KY: Turner Publishing Co., 1993), pp. 173-281.

[273] Ed[ward] Branigan to William B. Breuer, January 11, 1984. Coxey's Army was composed of a disheveled band of unemployed men, led by Jacob Coxey, who marched to Washington, D.C. on May 1, 1894, following the financial Panic of 1893. Coxey's Army of some 500 marchers, the first significant popular protest in the capital in U.S. history, petitioned Congress to create jobs such as building roads and improving public works as measures to relieve the recent wave of unemployment and poverty.

For much of the next month, we moved about locally, maintaining a stronghold over the region. For part of this month, we were assigned to guard a railroad bridge. On April 22, we in the 464th front echelon returned to Wesel and assumed security guard duty for this city. Our rear echelon was sent to Hamborn, Germany. According to Branigan, our assigned duties included the "feeding of displaced persons" (i.e., the French, Russians, and other nationalities in this area). We were also designated to "control the[ir] movement and evacuation." As we had not been pushed forward with the rest of the 17th Division, we often felt that we in Branigan's Bastard Battalion might, at any time, be detached from the rest of the division.

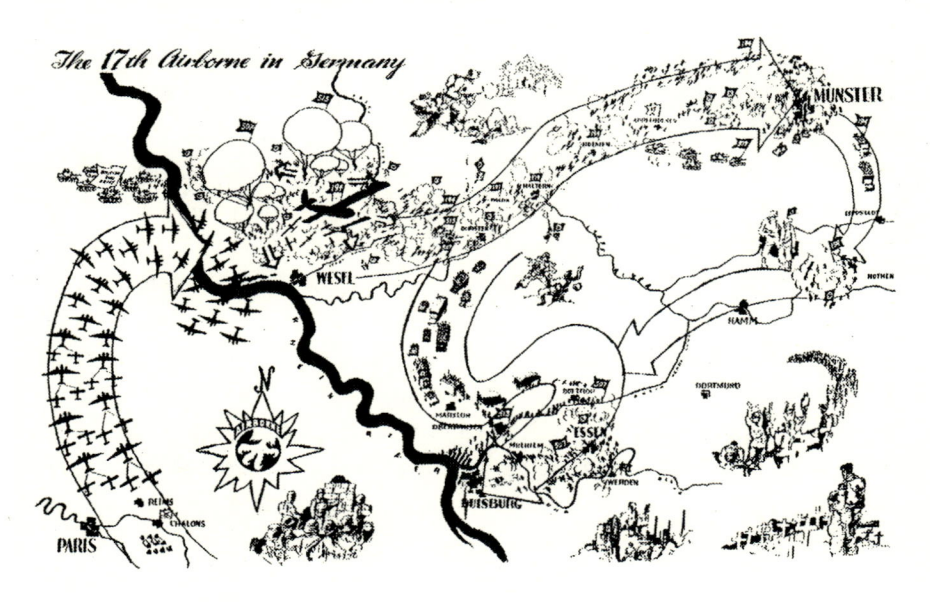

During this time, when off duty, we journeyed into the remains of Wesel for recreation. We played a lot of baseball, softball, and pitched horse shoes. Only a few in our battalion bragged of their battle activity. By and large, we knew that we were there to do our job, and we knew that completing the mission depended more upon the actions (and survival) of the whole force than upon any individuals. We sensed that we, as an army, were winning the war. So, we remained focused on what still must be done to get this war over with as soon as possible so that we could get back home. We interacted well with our infantry counterparts in the neighboring camps. Our mutual combat experience had brought us much closer together than we had been back in the States. No longer did infantry – vs – artillery fights occur at the frequency they once had in stateside beer gardens.

Looting was commonplace, though I only knew of it on a small scale. Soon after our drop we had been given some of our pay in Deutsch Marks (our "Invasion Currency") to pay for our needs. Still, nearly everyone that I knew picked up an item or two as a "souvenir" of our time in Germany. As Glen Gray described in The Warrior, souvenirs "give the soldier some assurance of his future beyond the destructive environment of the present." For the soldier, they "represented a promise that he might survive."[274] We were aware that we had to carry everything we looted in our duffel bag. I kept my eye out for a few pocket-sized items every now and then. I had picked up a sword on one occasion, but later determined that since I could not carry it concealed in the duffle bag, I had better leave it behind. I did secure a P-38 pistol and an old cap – and – ball pistol. These items, representative of German warfare history, were much easier to pack away and carry. One machinist that I knew picked up a tool box and filled it all along the way with German micrometry tools – the very best of such tools at the time.

I never took any leave time while in Germany, although others did. Once, when a soldier I hardly knew was heading off to Paris, I sent two rolls of film with him to have them developed. When he returned, he said that he had lost them, but I never believed that son of a bitch. Someone else may still have my snaps of our battlefield, the Rhine, and Wesel in their own family's army album.

As cooks, we were still in charge of feeding the troops. By D+3, we had set up temporary cooking facilities that had been trucked in to us. This timing worked out quite nicely as we had jumped with only three days worth of C- and K-rations.[275] Provisions for our outfit were trucked in twice weekly after that time. Not having any refrigerators,

---

[274] As cited by Ambrose, Band of Brothers, p. 155.

[275] C-rations consisted of canned meat and vegetable units (M-units) including meat and beans, meat and vegetable hash, and meat and vegetable stew as well as hard biscuits and a powdered beverage package (B-units). The meat was typically a pork lunch meat loaf or a mixed pork and beef loaf. K-rations consisted of a fortified chocolate bar (generally from Hershey's Foods) that was designed to provide a high

we once again relied heavily upon dehydrated products. Spam had become our staple food.

Even when our provisions were adequate, we did not always have hot food for we had to first receive permission, day and night, to light our gas stoves so as not to give away our position. When we used fires, we tried to keep them concealed at all times. When possible, hot coffee and blister bags filled with water were generally available from the camp kitchen provided that the soldier brought his own cup or canteen.

None of the cooks in our battalion had been hurt, so we worked together in similar fashion to what we had in Camp Lucky Strike. Compared to the activity on and soon after our D-Day jump, it seemed that during the following weeks, we were really not doing as much as I thought that we might. This view, however, is from a cook's perspective. Those who pulled guard duty would likely have a very different view of the situation.

Unlike our experience at Camp Lucky Strike, there was nothing to be secured from nearby communities. The local German farmers may have hidden some food that, by now, they were forced to consume for sustenance, but the warfare had left them in quite desperate conditions. Although we did not view these farmers as enemy soldiers, we did not bother about their welfare at this time either.

One day we noticed some cattle wandering through the nearby pastureland that intermingled with our camp site. After some deliberation, all the while keeping our eye on a particular calf, we plotted our course to secure some fresh meat. Early the next morning, we dug a hole as we knew that we would need to bury the evidence. Stealing a calf was, after all, against military orders. A half dozen of us, including a fellow in the battalion who had knowledge of butchering, left camp early that morning, caught and slaughtered the calf, quickly cutting it up into portions useable for steak, hamburger, and stew. Everyone enjoyed having such fresh meat on this one occasion, and we quickly buried the remains.

---

energy meal during emergency situations. The breakfast K-rations also contained a fig bar laxative and a small packet of folded toilet paper, whereas the noon rations contained a tin of cheese. As John Magill observed in his <u>We Led From The Sky</u> (p. 54) "the "breakfast laxative was offset by the mid-day cheese."

A German farmer who must have owned the calf, came to talk with our troops, claiming that he was short one head of cattle. Everyone held to the story that "we know nothing about it." After a few days, a group of us decided to secure another calf. In the small herd of cattle, we spied a fine looking calf and kept coaxing it to stay around our campsite close to the kitchen, feeding it a little something special as we could. It was quite a tame animal, and it soon came to us without any hesitation. However, having already lost one animal, the German farmer was also keeping a close eye on that calf as well as on us. After a short while, he would come to retrieve his calf, but it would eventually return. Still, despite our strong desire for more fresh meat, we never did slaughter that calf. For once, we adhered to the warnings that we had received from our supervisors against butchering any more of the German livestock.

On one occasion, a verbal fight arose from the kitchen, between Sergeant La Coste and Corporal Truelove. Truelove was demoted and sent to lug ammunition, and I was promoted to a Corporal T-5. This "T" (i.e., Technician) rating was "common among technicians, cooks, and bandsmen" during the war.[276] La Coste and I got along just fine. I've always considered this incident to be my "battlefield commission" as it had taken place on what was our field of battle.

One other incident that comes to mind regards moonshine. Once as some of our men were talking about their pre-war experiences in making moonshine, we in the kitchen realized that we just might have the necessary ingredients. After all, we had dried fruit, potatoes, sugar, and yeast as well as the requisite cookery utensils. So, we mixed up a batch and started this mash soaking in a five-gallon GI gas can that we had scoured with boiling water. In order to keep our activities private, we set this recipe cooking on the upper floor of an abandoned house nearby. Fermentation was under way, and the previously dented can soon smoothed itself and began to swell. This all happened much more quickly than we had planned, so we secured two more cleaned out five-gallon cans and divided the contents of the one into the other two, all the while keeping a close eye on the "growth" of these cans.

---

[276] John Andrews, <u>Airborne Album 1943-1945 Normandy to Victory</u> (Williamstown, NJ: Phillips Publications, c.1992), p. 2.

After a few days, we talked over what we should do next. We found two empty five-gallon tin cans that had previously contained our kitchen-sized helping of food provisions, and we cleaned them up a bit. In need of copper tubing, we went to look over some wrecked planes and vehicles. Although no copper tubing was to be found, we did secure some other metal tubing. Now, we had to adapt the tubing so that it would attach to our two containers. We 'borrowed' two metal funnels from the kitchen and, after dividing the souring mash between the containers, we soldered the funnels upside down onto each container's open end. Finally, we had a satisfactory device, and we set it slowly burning over a small wood fire.

Not being experts in the moonshine business, we never did know quite what would happen next. We could tell that the two five-gallon cans were "breathing," swelling back and forth over the flame of the fire. We thought that soon it would either explode or, as we hoped, start dripping from the end of the coils that we had attached to the pointed ends of the funnels. The only thing to do now was to wait and watch.

After several hours of watching the can "breathe" over the fire, we saw a drip come off the ends of one of the two coils. We placed a glass under the coil to catch it, and it continued to drip, albeit very slowly. We stuck our fingers in the glass, tasting the product of our labors. The more it dripped, the better it tasted. We let it drip all night long, collecting a good pint from each of the containers. Although we had no way of knowing what percentage alcohol we had created, it sure was powerful.

After we got all that we could get out of this apparatus, we trashed our machine and never tried to make any more. The whole process took around two weeks, and it involved half a dozen fellows, including some from the Motor Pool who had supplied us with the solder. To my knowledge, the six of us kept this German moonshine adventure pretty well under wraps.

"Sure, colonel, I sell it—but you gotta bring your own jug."

On May 8, while camped in Wesel, what had been "the Reich's last western rampart," we heard the news of the end of the war in Europe.[277] This was, as one Divisional history recalls, "good" but "expected" news.[278] The news of victory over Europe, what became known as VE Day, meant great things about the U.S., and it also reframed my perspective on the Germans from that point in time.

---

[277] Pay, <u>Thunder From Heaven</u>, p. 36. For an overview of the reactions to this day from various perspectives, see Martin Gilbert, <u>The Day the War Ended: May 8, 1945 – Victory in Europe</u> (New York: Holt, 1995).

[278] F. Langston and J. Buckridge, <u>Talon Crosses the Rhine</u>, May 8 – V.E. Day section.

TALON

17th AIRBORNE DIVISION NEWSMAGAZINE

ONE JOB DONE
(SEE PAGE 5)

VOLUME I   JUNE 15, 1945   NUMBER 1

Early after landing, we had remained somewhat leery of German civilians. A German was a German; they were all our enemies. This fear dissipated as time passed, and an openness between our troops and the Germans expanded even more following VE Day. Although I was not entirely trusting of them, I was willing to try to be friendly. After all, the German people without Hitler may not be entirely tainted with a Nazi–laden future.

Most of the Germans that I met following VE Day had willingly accepted defeat, and they were glad to be through with the fighting. We did not, however, drop our weapons and go and hug them as has often been depicted of Allied soldiers and their enemies at the news of the armistice signing that had ended World War I. However, I did not believe that holding feelings of animosity toward them would do any of us any good any longer.

After VE Day, U.S soldiers accepted a new mission to help the civilians, as well as the displaced nationals, back into whatever remained of their homelands. After interrogating the families still around Wesel, they were allowed to return home, or to where their homes had once been. We tried to help these people the best we could for immediate needs, but their long term care soon became critical.

Food was of utmost concern. General Miley's directive issued three weeks before VE Day had made that point clear to the Germans. "Your armies," he admonished them, have "wantonly destroyed food stocks in other countries as they were forced to retreat." You then "forced citizens of other countries to come here to work on farms and in factories" for your war efforts. "You brought in the Displaced Person for your gain" so "you and not the Allies must now feed them." As part of our service, "we intend to see that you do." "If there is not sufficient food for all," then "only the Displaced Persons will eat." If "you do not feed them," then "we will let them take what they need." Your retreating soldiers have wrecked "almost every bridge in Germany," thereby transportation has become "paralized [sic] making food distribution difficult if not impossible."[279] Miley directed the Germans in the area under the

---

[279] W.M. Miley. "Directive to Germans in the area under control of the 17th Division, April 19, 1945," William M. Miley Papers, Box 2, "Miley, Official Correspondence, Sent. April 19-August 1, 1945," Folder, USAMHI. For more information on the German account of Operation Varsity and its aftermath, see Johann J. Nitrowski, Die Luftlandung und das Kriegsende im Gebiet der Städte Hamminkeln und Wesel (Hamminkeln: Stadt Hamminkeln, 1997), and Alexander Berkel, Krieg vor der Eigenen Haustür: Rheinübergang und Luftlandung am Niederrhein 1945, Studien und Quellen zur Geschichte von Wesel 17 (Wesel: Stadtarchivs Wesel, 1994).

control of his 17th Division to: 1) immediately direct everyone in your district to grow food stocks; 2) immediately start work with a view to repair power, water, and transportation facilities; and 3) get together right now and unselfishly decide how one section of the country can help another. He reminded them that the "rural districts will need coal badly next winter and if they don't start getting it now[, then] the limited transportation left you by Hitler and his brigands will prevent its distribution when everyone needs it at the same time." Similarly, "the cities will need food badly when winter comes," thus you "should be stocking it now." As one final suggestion, Miley urged the locals to "Start advocating peace in every way you can." The "millions" of POWs now held by the Allies would not, he argued, be returned "until peace is declared."[280]

Following VE Day, we supplied the local people with what gifts of supplies we could – coffee, sugar, cigarettes, blankets – as an extension of friendship. In the end, these families had shown themselves to be trustworthy. Like many other soldiers after the VE period in this area, I became pretty well acquainted with the German families that we helped resettle. In one of these families, I became attracted to a particular fräulein, and we saw quite a bit of each other despite my having been told by superiors to avoid fraternizing.

After the fighting, I, like many other GIs, began to see the good in the hearts of German peoples. We were sorry that we had had to fight, but fighting had been necessary to overpower that dictator. They, like we, had fought courageously for a cause. General Eisenhower acknowledged that the Germans had fought with courage, but "courage was not enough. Reinforcements failed to arrive, weapons, ammunition and food alike ran short, and the dearth of fuel caused their powers of tactical mobility to dwindle to [a] vanishing point." In the "last stages of the campaign," the Germans could, so the Supreme Commander of the Allied Expeditionary Forces argued, "do little more than wait for the Allied avalanche to sweep them over."[281]

---

[280] W.M. Miley, "Directive to Germans in the area under control of the 17th Division," April 19, 1945.

[281] Dwight D. Eisenhower, Supreme Commander, Allied Expeditionary Force, "Report on Operations in Northwest Europe, 6 June 1944 – 8 May 1945," p, 117, USAMHI.

Chapter 6:

Gathering the Chute – Activity after Varsity

Perhaps someday these things will be a pleasure to recall.

William F. Whipps, Paratrooper

<u>Reflections After Varsity</u>

After having taken off twelve times in an airplane, I realized that I had never actually landed in an airplane – I had always walked back after jumping. After that twelfth jump, the jump across the Rhine – my only jump in combat – I was just so very grateful that I was able to walk back at all.

Both the forward and rear echelons of the 464th Battalion departed Wesel on June 15, arriving and setting up camp in Neufchateau, France two days later. This trip included time aboard trains as well as being hauled in army transport trucks. While camped in Neufchateau, I reported to sick call that my throat was bothering me. After they inspected my condition, they wanted to send me to the hospital to have my tonsils removed. However, I did not want to be separated from my battalion which was now on the move. I feared that by spending time in the hospital, I would not be able to rejoin my brothers for any future activity that they were to encounter. I was unaware that, as Ambrose reported, "Airborne policy" stipulated the "return [of] recovered men to their original company."[282]

Over the course of a month that summer, we saw many wounded soldiers being tended to around our camp. I never thought of the wounded as being "lucky," in their having a ticket home while I was still facing potential death on the battlefield. Rather, I thought that they, like me, were there doing a job, but misfortune hit them. I hated to see anyone wounded from war injuries, no matter what side of the conflict they fought for. Some people did talk of the wounded as "lucky dogs," but I never saw it that way.

While growing up in Kansas, I had seen a number of veterans who had been gassed during World War I who carried their breathing apparatuses with them. As a kid, I thought that they seemed a bit odd, as did the peg-legged and one armed veterans of that conflict. However, once we learned of their war efforts, we thought differently about them.[283] Still, at the time, we could not begin to appreciate or understand the hurt that they had gone through. After my own experiences in war, however, I now had a much more humble and helpful approach towards dealing with the many disabled veterans that I encountered.

After a month, we departed Neufchateau on July 13, officially departing the 17th Airborne Division at that time as well. We were scheduled for redeployment as part of the airborne invasion of Japan. We arrived at another "Cigarette Camp," Camp Twenty Grand in

---

[282] Ambrose, <u>Band of Brothers</u>, p. 109.

[283] Disabled Veterans of various historical eras are becoming one of the focal points of investigation in the burgeoning field of academic literature devoted to Disability Studies. See, for instance, David T. Mitchell and Sharon L. Snyder (eds) <u>The Body and Physical Difference: Discourses of Disability</u> (Ann Arbor, MI: University of Michigan Press, 1997).

France on July 15, then, on August 4, we left the Le Havre, France Port of Embarkation aboard the U.S.A.T. Sea Porpoise.

U.S.A.T. Sea Porpoise

Built in 1944 by the Ingalls Shipbuilding Corporation in Pascagoula, Mississippi, the U.S.A.T Sea Porpoise was a C3 type freighter–turned troopship operated during WWII by the United States Lines Company. At 492 feet in length, this 7,934 gross ton ship was outfitted for 2,636 passengers. The Sea Porpoise had just completed two trips of carrying troops from Le Havre to New York at the average speed of 16 and ½ knots. For the third voyage in this series of trips, she had left New York on July 25.

The 464th PFAB was the first to board and, according to custom, the first to board pulled extra duty in helping the Navy crew throughout the voyage. I headed for the kitchen where I was assigned to help clean, serve, and cook. We ate a lot of beans on that trip, but we also had quite a bit of fruit. This fruit had been frozen to help preserve it until we were ready to serve it at meals.

Cooking for thousands, as compared to the hundred that I had cooked for since arriving at Camp Mackall, was challenging. The amount of food we prepared on the Sea Porpoise at one time was drastically different in comparison. The men aboard ship ate in shifts pretty much throughout the day, and I helped during most of these meal times. At least it gave me something to do. Many others aboard just killed time as we sailed for New York.

The ship itself, as John F. Magill recounted, was so "crammed to the rafters" that the troopers nicknamed it the "Packed Porpoise." Magill recalls that the sea was rough – so much so that troopers were found everywhere hanging over the rails, over the commodes, and over the waste receptacles.[284]

Like a few other guys aboard ship, I noticed that I had developed a serious rash and itch. I reported to sick call and was found to have scabies (the "red itch"). With a doctor's permit, I was allowed to take fresh water showers, in addition to my medical treatment, whereas everyone aboard ship typically took salt water showers.

While aboard the Sea Porpoise, late on August 6, we heard the announcement over the loud speakers of the atomic bomb drop over Hiroshima. "None of us on board had any idea what an atomic bomb was, but by its power, when compared to the British blockbuster, we all knew that the world was launched into a whole new era. The news of Russia joining forces against Japan was pleasing, though it seemed quite belated to us."[285]

As we had completed our European missions, we were informed that we were going to report back to Camp Mackall from where, after returning from a thirty-day leave, we would head out for the Pacific Theatre. We arrived in New York on August 13, after just a week at sea with smooth waters at the end of the journey. The Statue of Liberty never looked so good. We were housed for one night at Camp Kilmer, New Jersey, leaving there on August 14, and arriving back in Camp Mackall on the following day, August 15. All went very well on that journey. We thought, "What the Hell. The War in Europe is over. We were back in the States alive, and we were on our way to a 30-day leave

---

[284] Magill, <u>We Led From the Sky</u>, p.86.
[285] Magill, <u>We Led From the Sky</u>, p. 87.

to go home." We celebrated being back in the States aboard the train en route to Mackall. We pooled our ready cash and gave it to one of our boys. He jumped off our very slow moving train to find us some drinks – beer, liquor, anything he could buy. As he came running back, we helped him aboard our train car. He had succeeded in this mission, and the partying began.

It was a great feeling to be back on familiar grounds as we arrived at Camp Mackall. But it was to be even a more glorious day than we could have imagined. For later that day, August 15, we learned in a radio broadcast of the U.S. victory over Japan. Emperor Hirohito had accepted the U.S. terms of an unconditional surrender. Celebrations continued at camp and off base.

From this time on, although still in the Army, I never pulled any other duties – no more cooking! We soon received our traveling orders and were on our way back home. Another trooper of the 464th PFAB, James E. "Jimmie" Higgins, from Wichita, Kansas joined me on the road, and we made a good traveling pair.

I had never been to Wichita before. However, I had a twin sister, Roberta Lois (Wilson) F, who lived there, and she had a place for me to stay anytime that I was in town. Most of my time over the next two weeks, I bussed and hitchhiked between the south eastern Kansas communities of Wichita, Douglass, Elk City, Independence, and Chanute, getting reacquainted with my family and friends. While in the Army, my family had moved from Elk City to Douglass, Kansas so that my father could more easily bus to his job of gardening and caretaking for a number of families in Wichita throughout the week, and then returning home on the weekends. Jimmie Higgins and I began living life the only way we knew how to at the time – to eat, drink (especially drink), and be merry. We always had a place to stay and plenty to eat. Our accommodations were always to our satisfaction.

Roberta Lois (Wilson) and Ralph Bowers

One day we reviewed our traveling orders and found that we were to have reported to Fort Leavenworth on that very day, but we were still in Wichita, some two hundred miles away. We headed to the railroad station, made the appropriate train connections, and arrived in Leavenworth. However, as we arrived, we saw a departing train – our train – bound for North Carolina. We were not officially AWOL, but we had missed our train. We reported to the area where we should have been some twelve hours earlier, but the personnel there in the Company Charge of Quarters (C.Q.) did not know what to do with us. They eventually secured a place for us to eat and sleep that night, and we reported back to them the next morning as instructed.

That next morning, the C.Q. officer had about an hour-long chat with us. Then, after reviewing our traveling orders, he asked whether we could use a seven-day pass. So, with our new traveling orders in our pockets, we headed back to Wichita. Our friends there now thought we had gone AWOL, but after showing them our orders, we rejoined in celebrating life much the same as we had done before.

We returned to Leavenworth in time to catch our scheduled train to North Carolina. Back in Camp Mackall, we rejoined those of the 464th that were still there, but it was a strikingly different ambience. We were all herded around and around as if the Army did not quite know what to do with us. With so many soldiers having returned stateside, the Army had to do something with us and to keep track of our whereabouts as the process of being discharged slowly took effect. With my name being "Wilson," and the Army working alphabetically, I was at the tail end of the line for discharge. Not being a "high pointer," I knew that I had a considerable wait ahead.

We had virtually no obligations throughout each day. Although we kept to a regular reveille – to – taps schedule, with normal meal times, we – the fittest of the fit among the Army's elite forces – did not even have to do any calisthenics. All in all, we did a hell of a lot of nothing.

Winter came along and we learned that we were going to be sent to Ft. Bragg, North Carolina, some forty miles from Camp Mackall. As I approached those in charge, I was asked, considering my points and service, would I like a 45-day delay en route. I said, "Sure!"

Before I had gone overseas, I had met a family in Salisbury, N.C. – a man, his wife, and their 20-year-old daughter. We had maintained correspondence with each other throughout my time overseas. Now, with a 45-day leave, winter setting in, and no money in my pockets, I called upon them. So, for the next forty five days, we grew very close to each other.

At the end of this leave, I reported to Ft. Bragg for my final duties. I received my final traveling orders, a trip to Ft. Leavenworth. There, on January 31, after 2 years, 11 months, and 14 days of [U.S.] Continental service and 6 months and 3 days of Foreign service, I received an Honorable Discharge from my military service of the United States of America. While we were being mustered out of the service at Ft. Leavenworth, I reported that I was owed some back pay. This payment was arranged, and I also informed them of my desire to, at last, have my tonsils removed. This, too, was arranged, and papers were drawn up that were usable at any Veterans Administration (VA) hospital. I followed through with this surgery later in the summer of 1946 in the VA hospital back in Wichita, Kansas.

A little more than a year out of the Army, I thought quite a bit about going back into the services. At that time, I wanted to apply for the Fire Jumpers unit that was fighting the fires in Idaho, Montana, and Oregon that were rampant.[286] I had the jump experience, and it seemed a natural way to put it back into further use for my country. One group of men from Mackall that I had known before we left for Europe, the 'Triple Nickels' (the 555th Parachute Infantry Battalion), had gone to Oregon on May 5, 1945. This battalion, the U.S.'s first all black battalion, became the country's first Military Parachute Fire Fighting Unit, more commonly known as the Airborne Smoke Jumpers.[287]

At times I have wondered just why I did not continue this parachute work. Most likely, it was a blossoming love life that turned me against this pathway. I had met a young lady, Margaret Guyot, in the grocery store that her father owned in Douglass, Kansas, and we were making our own life plans. It did not seem that I should add this stress to married life when other, less hazardous, options for work were also readily available. Looking back over the forty-four years of married bliss with Margaret before her death in October 1992, I certainly made the right decision for my life.

Reflections upon Operation Varsity

In retrospect, U.S. Paratroopers of World War II "fought under tremendous handicaps." The planes they flew in were not capable of carrying heavy equipment, thus the troopers "had to make up for it in fighting spirit." A paratrooper's artillery was "of the lightest type; and

---

[286] Norman Maclean provides an engaging, though tragic, story of fire jumpers in Young Men and Fire (Chicago: The University of Chicago Press, 1992).
[287] One of these Airborne Smoke Jumpers, Bradley Biggs, recounted the history of this unit in The Triple Nickels: America's First All-Black Paratroop Unit (Hamden, CT: Archon Books, 1986).

the only ground transport that he had was what could be brought in by glider." A paratrooper had "no tanks, no construction equipment, and no anti-aircraft support. In short, he had it tough!"[288]

Curiously, post-Operation accounts of the importance of the Varsity assault varied widely. One historian called it "the most spectacular but perhaps least known great airborne feat of the war – in fact, of all subsequent wars." It succeeded with "near flawless execution." It was, claimed the author of <u>Ridgway's Paratroopers</u>, the "first letter-perfect airborne operation of the war."[289] Another military historian speculated that the "drop across the Rhine" would be "a feat . . . remembered by historians as one of the truly great military maneuvers of all time."[290] The conduct of this Operation "demonstrated a level of maturity in the planning and execution of airborne warfare."[291] Its success "underscored the accelerating collapse of Nazi Germany and a rising confidence in victory for the Allies in western Europe."[292]

Soon after Operation Varsity, General Brereton, in a letter to General Ridgway written in a style characteristic of many commanders who lauded the success of operations under their command, praised Varsity as "a triumph of successful planning, rigorous training and faultless execution of which every officer and man may well be proud." He continued his memo noting that the "arrival of your divisions in the right place at the right time, and the outstanding gallantry with which they fought" had "contributed in large measure to the success" of the Rhine crossing and "to the sweeping exploitation now in progress." All ranks, Brereton concluded, "acquitted themselves superbly and *in the finest airborne tradition*."[293] (Authors' emphasis) General Eisenhower noted that the "brilliant results" of Varsity "reflected the great strides made in this [Airborne] aspect of warfare since the landings made on D-Day, nine months earlier."[294]

---

[288] Bradley and Wood, <u>Paratrooper</u>, no pagination.

[289] Blair, <u>Ridgway's Paratroopers</u>, p. 449.

[290] Hagerman, "Operation Varsity," p.137.

[291] Bilstein, <u>Airlift and Airborne Operations in World War II</u>, p. 38.

[292] Bilstein, <u>Airlift and Airborne Operations in World War II</u>, p. 38.

[293] L.H. Brereton to M.B. Ridgway, April 3, 1945, William M. Miley Papers, Box 2, "Miley, Official Correspondence between Gen. Brereton and Gen. Ridgway," Folder, USAMHI.

Yet, as Barry Gregory and others have argued, Operation Varsity was "not entirely necessary." The Allied airborne troops "successfully accomplished their tasks[,] but their success did not justify the [heavy] losses."[295] The losses within the two airborne divisions during Varsity were "greater than that suffered by the 82nd and 101st [Airborne Divisions] on the first day of the Normandy invasion."[296] It was, others have deemed, "far too costly."[297] The "waste" incurred by Varsity was considered by some as "fearsome" and "desperately costly" as it "absorb[ed] disproportionately large amounts of badly needed resources for a return which at best was transitory."[298]

Even Charles B. MacDonald's official account reported in the United States Army in World War II claimed "there was no need for Operation Varsity." The "capture of the high ground east of the Rhine could have been done at less cost by ground troops" and that "no gain" was obtained from the airborne landings accelerating the "speed of construction of the Rhine bridges."[299]

Official records list the "overall cost of Varsity" as "moderate." Seven British troop carriers were destroyed as well as 46 American aircraft, though nine were salvaged, and 15 bombers were lost during the resupply mission. Up to the beginning of D+3, the 17th Division amassed a total of 231 of their number dead and 670 wounded, and 6th Airborne casualties on D-Day amounted to 346 dead, 731 wounded and 319 missing, although many later rejoined their units.[300] Such loses were balanced by great gains. According to General Ridgway, during the six days between March 24 and 30, while advancing over seven miles per day on average, 8000 prisoners were taken. The enemy's entire 84th Infantry Division was "destroyed" and "at least 124 artillery and anti-aircraft pieces and 26 tanks were taken."[301]

---

[294] "Supreme Commanders Dispatch for Operations in Northwest Europe," p. 97.

[295] Gregory, United States Airborne Forces, p. 124.

[296] Don Lassen and Richard K. Schrader, Pride of America: An Illustrated History of the U.S. Airborne Forces (Missoula, Montana: Pictorial Histories Publishing Co., 1991), p. 31.

[297] Mitchell, "Epilogue. One Last Great Jump," p. 254.

[298] Hickey, Out of the Sky, p.182.

[299] United States Army in World War II, as cited by Crookenden, Airborne at War, p.143.

[300] USAF Airborne Operations, pp. 90-91.

By all accounts, Varsity marked many historical points in airborne warfare. "Never again," would "entire divisions be committed in airborne warfare, never again would gliders be employed, and never again would the ill-fated C-46 be used to ferry paratroopers."[302]

Some of those who fought in Varsity, however, drew different conclusions. Crookenden, for example, summarized the powerful events of March 24 as they affected the outcome of the war. Two entire airborne divisions successfully "captured 4,000 prisoners — and probably killed and wounded another thousand" that single day. German General Fiebig later confirmed that all 4,000 men of his 84th Infantry Division had been "eliminated almost to a man" and that "most of the Karst Group were also destroyed."[303] Even more important was the complete destruction of "90 German artillery pieces, ranging from 155 mm down to 76 mm" together with "a large number of 20 mm guns in multiple mountings and hundreds of machine guns." It "seems likely," Crookenden concluded," that the "undisturbed fire power of these guns might well have held up the advance from the Rhine of the assault divisions . . . and delayed the construction of the bridges," ultimately delaying the end of the war.[304]

Many of the U.S. Army's official reports and congratulatory letters exchanged between members of the high command recalled Operation Varsity in glowing, victorious language. XVIII Corps Commander Ridgway praised the "strategic and tactical doctrine" governing the use of Airborne forces in Operation Varsity, and suggested that it "serve as a model for future airborne operations."[305] He highlighted the combat performance of the 17th Airborne Division in a March 29 letter to General Miley, assuring him that the Division "has fully measured up to my expectations" and had, "*in all respects, maintained the superior standards set by other airborne divisions in prior operations.*"[306] (Authors' emphasis)

---

[301] Matthew B. Ridgway, "An Airborne Corps Operation," <u>Military Review</u> 25 (1945): 16.

[302] Mitchell, "Epilogue. One Last Great Jump," p. 254.

[303] Crookenden, <u>Airborne at War</u>, p. 144.

[304] Crookenden, <u>Airborne at War</u>, p. 144.

[305] XVIII Corps (Airborne) Operation Varsity 23 March, 1945 to 30 March 1945, p. 12.

Lt. Colonel Lloyd R. Moses, who was attached to the 17th Division during the Wesel-Haltern area campaign, applauded the Division's "morale and fighting spirit in all ranks," and claimed the "degree to which new reinforcements," including the 464th, had been indoctrinated was "superior to any I had seen."[307] In another complimentary letter, Major General John B. Anderson noted Miley's work in the varied missions of the late Varsity assault to have been successfully executed "with a minimum of means." The defensive and offensive missions and the organization of a "highly populated area" were successful in containing not only a "large enemy population, but also great numbers of displaced persons." The "clearing of Essen" was noted to have been accomplished with "prompt and speedy action of the division."[308]

Thus, according to one level of acknowledgement, the 17th Airborne Division was widely recognized at the time for their successful operation in crossing the Rhine. Later accounts, however, talk of the 17th Division as the "Forgotten Airborne Division."[309]

---

[306] M.B. Ridgway to W.M. Miley, March 29, 1945, William M. Miley Papers, Box 2, "Miley, Official Correspondence, Received. January 24-July 26, 1945," Folder, USAMHI.

[307] Lloyd R. Moses to W.M.Miley, April 22, 1945. William M. Miley Papers, Box 2, "Miley, Offical Correspondence, Received. January 24-July 26, 1945," Folder, USAMHI.

[308] J.B. Anderson to W.M. Miley, April 24, 1945. William M. Miley Papers, Box 2, "Miley, Offical Correspondence, Received. January 24-July 26, 1945," Folder, USAMHI.

[309] Bart Hagerman, for example, comments on this in his "The 17th Airborne Division . . . 'WWII's Forgotten Troopers'," The Airborne Quarterly 15(2002): 151-152.

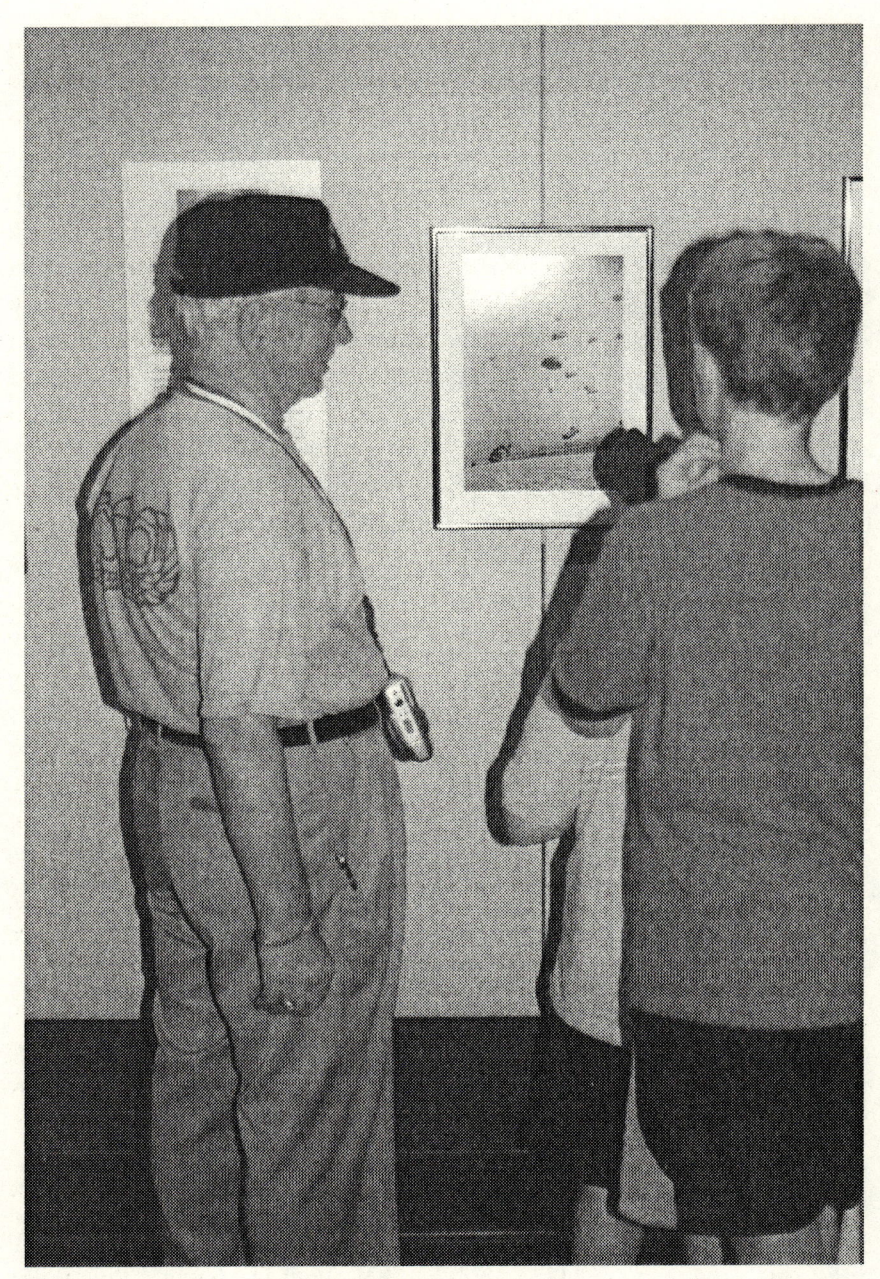

Robert Wilson Explaining Rhine Jump to Grandsons, James and Doug Wilson, Smithsonian Institution, Memorial Day Weekend, 2004

John Andrews dubbed Varsity as World War II's "Forgotten Finale." This lack of attention, he claimed, resulted in large part due to "the glare of publicity for Patton's armored juggernauts engaged down south" along the Rhine.[310] When all of the other airborne divisions had disbanded, "Jumping Jim" Gavin led his 82nd Airborne Division through a ticker tape parade on January 12, 1946 shortly after their return to the States. No mention was made of the 17th Division during this celebration other than its unique group of troopers, the all-black battalion, the 555th – a strong battalion to be sure, but a battalion that never left the United States.[311]

Despite having been involved in three major war campaigns and losing more of its men in the Rhine Drop, the "worst single day in Airborne history," the record of the 17th is often shown as paling in comparison to that of the 101st and the 82nd.[312] Perhaps, as John Kormann concluded, as this drop came "so close to the end of the war, one can understand why the military leadership wanted to gloss over 'Varsity' and its losses. Less understandable," he continues," is why military historians have not focused on it more or picked up on the definitive action that it was."[313]

On a more popular level, the 17th Division was not mentioned in the two popular movies that have dealt with exploits in which they were involved, "Battle of the Bulge" (1966) and "Patton" (1970). Another contributing factor to the diminished view of Varsity resulted from Montgomery's order for a 24-hour press blackout following the jump and a temporary withholding of information about the divisions involved in the Rhine crossing.[314]

The 17th Division, "Thunder From Heaven," actually became 'history' on September 16, 1945 as it was deactivated at Camp Myles Standish in Taunton, Massachusetts. Fortunately, however, the

---

[310] John Andrews, Airborne Album, pp. 67, 78.

[311] Gregory, United States Airborne Forces, p. 125. Although the 101st Airborne Division was disbanded for a time, it was reassembled as a parachute division on September 21, 1956.

[312] As Breuer reports in Geronimo (p. 558), on the Varsity D-Day, Miley's 17th Division suffered 159 men killed, 522 wounded, and 81 were missing.

[313] Kormann, "Another View of Operation Varsity," p. 13.

[314] Bart Hagerman, "Operation Varsity Airborne Bridge Across the Rhine," World War II 12 (1998): 52.

Division's history was already being recounted through a Divisional newsmagazine entitled <u>The Talon</u> that had began publication in Essen on June 15, 1945. Captain Don R. Pay, public relations officer of the 17th Division, was chiefly responsible for this publication and, in 1947, when back in the States, he assembled this work into an even larger Divisional history as <u>Thunder From Heaven: Story of the 17th Airborne Division 1943-1945</u>. First published in 1947, it has been reprinted two times. Still, no further attempt to recount the exploits of the entire Divisional history has been undertaken. History, of course, is always open to rewriting from new perspectives. As grist for the mill for future historians, many vignettes, including contributions from WW II veterans, may be gleaned from the pages of "Thunder From Heaven: The Official Bulletin of the 17th Airborne Division Association."

Who and what gets recorded in history often reflects the biases and specific interests of the authors. On one level, it is clear that the actions of the 17th Airborne in WW II have been slighted in historical accounts of what part we played in Allied war efforts. Furthermore, when one actually finds an account of the 17th Airborne, the efforts of the 464th PFAB, and indeed Raff's entire 507th Combat Team, have also been relatively unexplored. According to many accounts, including that of Lt. Col. Branigan, commanding officer of the 464th, it remains unclear as to "why Col. Raff, his 507th [Parachute Infantry Regiment] and my [Branigan's] 464th, never seemed to enjoy the favor of Div [ision] Headquarters." Indeed the "down grading of their accomplishments" is even evident in Pay's "official" public history of the 17th Airborne Division, <u>Thunder From Heaven</u>. Branigan concluded that, in part, this under appreciation stemmed from his own military background. For unlike all of the other major unit commanders of the 17th Division, Branigan was not a West Pointer. Branigan, however, should not have downgraded his own image at all. He was a courageous, meritorious, and decorated commander. Although we in the 17th Division may not have received the noteworthy mention of our achievements as did our brother troopers in the 101st and 82nd Divisions, it matters very little to those who were there. We all know very well what we endured and accomplished in achieving our missions on the battlefield. At the end of the day, that knowledge alone is enough consolation.

Paratroopers continue to hold their place in popular culture. Perhaps the best early post-war indication of this popularity is the success of the book, Those Devils in Baggy Pants. This memoir recounts the adventures of paratrooper Ross S. Carter in the 504th Parachute Regiment, part of Major General James Gavin's 82nd Airborne Division. This book, published in 1951, sold over a million copies and was later published as a Reader's Digest condensed book.[315] The author, himself, had died of cancer in 1947, and thus acknowledgements are also due to his brother, a college professor, who completed the memoir and helped bring it to light five years later.

In 1995, I retuned to what had been part of the ETO. I was very impressed by my visit to the city of Koln. It was meaningful to see how the Germans had kept a section of the city the way that it had looked following the Allied destruction of the city. Amidst the hustle of a modern city, another site – the two towers of Koln Cathedral – remains daunting. These towers had been intentionally untouched during the bombing raid over Koln so that they might serve as an architectural beacon from the ground, providing coordinates for U.S. and Allied air corps to better map their position.

From Koln, I went to Munster, where Philip participated in a history conference. While there, I noticed a considerable amount of building that had also gone up over the past half century. After a week in Munster, we rented a car and drove to Wesel. The city itself had been rebuilt mostly in red brick. An exhibit and diorama in the local church showed very vividly just how we had left the city in 1945. It brought a strong feeling of sadness to attend Sunday services in that church – a structure that itself still held pock marks of the bombing. A few other buildings had been preserved, all of which retained visible bomb holes that continued to serve as reminders of the past. Along the Rhine flowing nearby, the remains of destroyed bridges – remains that made those spots of the river look very familiar – continued to invoke a feeling of destruction. I touched some of these bridge remnants thinking back upon what we – the bridge and I – had witnessed here 50 years earlier. I also took a pleasure boat cruise along this section of

---

[315] Fortunately, this excellent memoir was republished in 1996, and is thus in print and available for a new generation of readers.

the Rhine. How ironic it felt to be reintroduced to the Rhine in a sense of pleasure. Of course it had once been somewhat pleasurable to know that what we, as soldiers, were doing at this site would actually bring a quicker end to the war.

Robert Wilson's Return to the Rhine, 1995

Robert Wilson in Reforested DZ Site, 50 Years Later

Plane Flying over our DZ Site, 50 years Later

With maps of the area from 1945 and 1995, we identified that area of Diersfordter Wald. The trees had certainly grown again, and the area that once served as our DZ had been transformed into a wheat field. I spent several hours wandering through this field and through the nearby, tall-treed forest. Curiously and eerily, while I was in the forest that had once been our DZ, a plane flew low overhead. Fifty years – so much of a lifetime that so many who died during the Rhine jump never had the opportunity to experience. I hope that I have led a life over the fifty-year interval of my having first visited this area in ways that those whose lives were snuffed out here would have respected. The emotions that filled me during my return to the DZ were among the most intense and varied that I've ever experienced.

It remains difficult to answer just why we, the U.S. forces, saw it as our responsibility to help Germany rebuild itself back up into a working economy. On a personal level, I supported these efforts. Peace – world peace – might be more readily obtained by such efforts. We tore up their lands, thus we should help them, during peaceful times, to put right what was once theirs.

The Germans did not fight on U.S. soil. Thus, those in the U.S. did not have that constant visual reminder that we, too, had had our families torn up by war. Those who do not believe that we should have helped our previous enemy rebuild its economy have been protected by not experiencing the day-to-day and year-to-year reconstruction of a country. Having returned to the site of our DZ, I was reminded once again of the extensive amount of necessary reconstruction. For many of us who had seen the destruction inflicted by U.S. soldiers, however, it was never difficult to feel the destruction that took place in far too many lives of our own countrymen.

In the years following the war, I came to forgive the Germans (and the Japanese and the Italians) for fighting against us. However, I have always remembered that they cost us in the U.S. many, many, many of our brothers, our family members, and our friends.

Robert Wilson at Parachute Panel, Opening Weekend of WWII Memorial, Washington, D.C.

Appendix:
List of the Members of the 464th Parachute Field Artillery Battalion

Extracted from D.R. Pay <u>Thunder From Heaven: Story of the 17th Airborne Division 1943-1945</u>, (Nashville: The Battery Press, 1947, Third Reprint Edition), pp. 90-179.

Abbott, Earl F.
Abbott, Herman F.
Abouaf, Isaac I., BS
Adams, Edgar L.
Agnew, Gerald L.
Albin, Harold L.
Alexander, Grady L., BS
Alexander, John C.
Alison, Julio J.
Allan, Edwin E.
Allen, John V.
Almeida, Joseph
Amiro, Albert
Anderson, David T.
Anderson, Frank A.

Antell, Ivan A.
Anthony, Rea J.
Ates, Gordon B.

Babb, Eugene R.
Baca, Florindo
Bailes, Ted
Baker, Willard
Balducci, Joseph
Barchenski, John J.
Barnes, Andrew P.
Barry, David R.
Barta, Edward W.
Baustian, Richard L.
Beard, Lowell N., KIA, SS
Beckwith, C. M., Jr.
Beconovich, Louis
Bellus, Albert B.
Bendowski, Chester J.
Berlin, Henry
Bertie, James F.
Bethea, Leonard A.
Bidwell, John E., KIA
Blanchard, Elmer D.
Boehme, Werner
Bonetti, Vincent
Borden, George M.
Boris, Nickolas
Bouthiette, Gerard N.
Bowers, James C.
Bowman, Ira A., Jr.
Bown, Teral N.
Boyer, Jack D.
Boyle, James A.
Boyles, Marvin F.
Bradley, Eugene M.

Branigan, Edward S., Jr., BS
Brantley, Earl N.
Bravo, Irving W., Jr.
Breithaupt, Oscar E., AM
Brennan, Dennis J.
Brock, Preston C.
Brohamer, Billie B.
Bromley, Edwin L.
Brooks, Charles S.
Brooks, John L.
Bruce, William B.
Buehler, Clyde W.
Buehler, Joseph F. G.
Bunch, Allie D.
Burch, Ben E.
Burger, Norbert J.
Burke, Clyde M.
Burns, John W., Jr.
Buswell, Gene R.
Butkus, Alfred B.
Byers, Charles G.

Caines, A. J.
Callender, Johnson
Campos, Jesse
Cardin, Raoul D.
Carter, Robert H.
Casey, Alfred W.
Castro, Benjamin C. Jr.
Chalmers, Luther
Chapman, Seymour
Charette, John F.
Charniga, John J.
Chlebowski, Joseph A.
Cirillo, Salvatore J.
Clift, Harold G.

Cohen, Sidney
Compton, George A.
Conner, George
Conner, James L.
Conroy, Patrick F.
Cooley, Boyd R.
Cooney, Jules W.
Crow, Louis C.
Crunk, Dock J.
Curtis, Joseph L.
Cope, Harold E.
Corcoran, Donald J.
Cordiero, John V.
Core, Charles M.
Cosentino, Vincent P.
Coughlin, W. E. Jr.
Coursey, Jack D.
Cousineau, Maurice G.
Craft, Henry J.

Dahnk, Anthony E.
Daniels, Dennis T.
Davie, William A.
Davis, Leon
Davis, Thomas M.
Davis, William B.
Dayton, Edward L.
Dean, George E. Jr.
Decker, Robert J.
Dekome, Ernest A.
De Mio, John J.
Deutsch, Joseph J., BS
Devoe, William J.
Dewar, Bruce B.
Dickens, Eugene G.
Dickey, Robert L.

Dill, Marvin R.
Di Michele, Anthony
Dionn, Anthony J.
Dobberstine, Thomas G.
Dolby, Francis M.
Dorn, Gale S.
Dorsey, John I. Jr.
Drawbridge, William J.
Dugan, Charles J.
Dunn, Nelson A.
Dyer, R. C.
Dyslin, Lyle A.

Edwards, L. C.
Edwards, William B.
Egelston, William R.
Egry, Alex
Ellis, Ernest W. Jr.
Engstrom, Earl L.
Erickson, Thorsten A.
Espe, Bernard L.
Esposito, Frederick
Esposito, Michael
Ethridge, Talmadge L
Ewan, Horace G.
Eynetich, John F.

Fadeley, Charles G.
Felix, Russell E.
Fields, Renis G.
Fillback, Harvey L., DOW, BS
Finley, Robert M.
Finnerty, John J., Jr.
Fisher, Robert
Flanaga, John E.

Fleischood, Gerald E.
Flores, Henry H.
Flynn, Robert A., BS
Folman, John W.
Ford, Felton
Foster, Mason
Fox, George M.
Frazier, Paul E.
Frenzilli, Roccas, Jr.
Freeze, Loyl H.
Frerk, Clair H.
Frey, Alfred C.
Fireson, Chester A.
Funk, William W.
Furtado, Anthony

Gabbard, Mike
Gallob, Joseph M.
Garcia, Alvaro
Garvin, Clarence E.
Gaston, Ralph A.
Gazdayka, Walter J.
Gaffken, Ralph W.
Gerhardt, Norman
Gerold, Joh H.
Gervais, Ralph R.
Gessleman, John M.
Getchell, Robert C.
Giacovelli, Leonard J.
Gibson, Robert L.
Gigas, Chester
Giles, William R.
Gillen, James J.
Gillespi, Bert F.
Gillespie, Albert P., BS
Gilley, Hollis C.

Glass, John F. Jr.
Goebel, Joel D.
Goodwin, William H., BS
Gordon, David
Gordon, Roy F.
Gorse, John W.
Gosnell, Walter R.
Gray, Oscar L. Jr.
Grimmett, Everett G., BS
Grubb, Robert L. Jr.
Guiles, Archie E. Jr.
Gurbacki Chester T.

Haecker, Christ A.
Haglund, Joseph H.
Hakkarainen, Sulo L.
Haley, Thestle L.
Hall, Harold K.
Hall, Manning J.
Halsey, James H.
Halstead, Earl B., KIA
Hamal, Joseph A., Jr.
Handy, Leroy
Harame, Theodore
Harding, Milton W.
Harris, Eugene T.
Hascup, Nelson
Hassler, William H.
Hatch, George F., Jr.
Hawkins, Jack B.
Hawley, George T.
Hayrynen, Jacob E.
Hays, William C.
Heath, Don E.
Heather, Roy E.
Hebert, Henry

Helmick, Calvin B.
Henry, Argo C.
Henry, Cephus
Henshaw, Francis S.
Hess, Gordon A.
Hewitt, Charles W.
Higgins, James E.
Hight, Donald H.
Hill, Athal H.
Hill, Marion F.
Hills, George E.
Hinds, Arthur C.
Hinson, Wade C.
Hipps, Robert R.
Hoffman, Paul A.
Hollis, Elmer Y., Jr.
Holser, Richard C.
Holupka, John M.
Horick, Pete, KIA (Although listed as 446, he should be either 464 or
    466.)
Horridge, Morrison E.
Horsechief, Alexander
Houser, Richard H.
Howland, Clark Jr.
Huey, Billy J.
Hunley, Harvey H.
Hunt, Walton E.
Hunter, John M.
Hynson, Duvall E.

Inskip, Leonard G.
Irby, Doyle L.
Irvin, Minyard E., BS
Isaacs, George E.
Isherwood, Thomas E.

Jackson, Lawrence H.
Jackson, Luther H.
Jackson, Vernon D.
Jacobs, Claude E., Jr.
Jasinski, Edward
Jean, Walton A.
Jee, Rolland
Jenkins, Marvis D.
Johnston, William D.
Jonas, James C.
Jones, John E.
Jones, Olin B.
Jones, Verna D.
Jones, Wallace R.
Joseph, Joseph
Jung, Eugene F. E. Jr.
Justice, Johnny H.
Jutrzonka, Anthony P.

Kasprzycki, Richard M.
Kelley, Richard G.
Kennedy, James L.
Kerney, Frank J.
Kerr, Clement E.
Kerrigan, John F.
King, Alonzo C.
Kinzeb, Fred W., Jr.
Kirby, Raymond D.
Kirkwood, Harry A.
Kissinger, Edmund L., KIA, BS
Klein, Derwood J.
Klein, James H.
Klesko, Thomas F.
Kopinski, Bruno A.
Kopp, Dean T.

Koring, Calvin J.
Korpalski, John E.
Kovachich, Michael
Krawczyk, Frank I.
Kubik, Charles
Kuchler, George A.

Labriola, Louis J.
Lach, John F.
La Coste, Edward W.
La Forte, James H.
Larkin, Edward H.
Law, Alexander
Lawhead, Don H.
Lawrence, James H.
Lawrence, Sam. H.
Leahey, Thomas F.
Lechlider, Charles E.
Lee, Raymond
Lemay, John
Lesh, Victor S.
Levergood, Daniel B.
Lewis, Eldon
Lewis, Robert D., II
Lieske, Charles H.
Lilly, Warren V.
Lindsey, Walter T.
Link, William F.
Liput, Edward G.
Lloyd, James R.
Loftice, James R.
Loftis James A.
Loggins, James L.
Long, Lawrence W.
Longawa, John A.
Loyd, Sam

Lucas, Raymond B.
Ludwig, Homer F.

McCaffery, Charles B.
McCarthy, Daniel E.
McCauley, Alfred R.
McCue, James P.
McCullough, Alfred A.
McCurdy, John J.
McDonald, Harvey W.
McDonnell, Henry
McGrew, Harry C.
McGuire, Pete
McIntosh, Billy G.
McKee, Hugh Jr.
McKenna, Don F.
McLane, George G.
Maciejewski, Chester
MacLean, Clarence Y.
Madaj, Frank J.
Madaline, Albert J.
Magill, John F., Jr.
Magolis, Frank
Malendoski, Arthur M.
Malter, Mario
Malinski, Walter T.
Mancinelli, Albert
Mandoli, Mario A.
Marcum, Jesse F.
Marez, Eugene B.
Marino, Louis J.
Markel, Robert S.
Marquez, Frank
Martin, Ernest
Martin, Willard E.
Martinson, Milo A.

Marvin, Ruel A.
Marx, Alvin R.
Matthews, Clifford J.
Matthews, Erich C., DOW
Maxwell, Douglas M.
Maye, Raymond F.
Mayhugh, Spencer A., Jr.
Mazurik, Frank R.
Meacham, Buck
Menowsky, Joseph A.
Meusel, Jack C.
Meyer, James H.
Miladinovich, Steve
Millard, Carl R.
Miller, Albert L.
Miller, Hugh M.
Miller, J. M.
Mills, Gordon G.
Milner, Frank T.
Misiak, Caimir J.
Moon, Anthony R.
Modzelewski, Edwin J.
Monroe, Walter E.
Moore, Lee P.
Moore, Louis C.
Moreno, Eugene
Moroney, Edward J.
Morris, Victor L.
Moses, Alpha
Motsinger, Dallas G.
Murphy, Hyrum H.
Musumeci, Valentie S.
Myatt, Edward C.

Nadeau, Jean P.
Nanni, Urindo

Napolitano, Carmine T.
Nase, Gerald F.
Naumchiek, Joseph J.
Neibauer, Herman G.
Nelson, Orval D.
Nelson, Robert P.
Netland, Richard E.
Nicholls, Robert G.
Nicholson, Maurice J.
Nierle, William A.
Noelte, Marlin S.
Norton, Ira B.
Nuzzi, Albert D.

O'Bryan, Harry L.
O'Laughlin, Leroy A.
Oneal, George E.
Oscipok, John
Osick,, Louis J.
Ostrander, Norman L.
Owens, Tolbert D.

Paci, Philip
Padgett, Herbert A.
Paloti, Andrew
Pandak, William L.
Parker, Walter C.
Pasek, Edwin S.
Patnode, Edward W.
Patrick, Frank R.
Patterson, John W.
Patterson, Roy A.
Paulauskas, Felix A.
Pease, James R.
Pena, Manuel M.

Pendley, Warren
Peoples, Joseph D., Jr.
Peterson, George P.
Peterson, Reuben W.
Pfendler, Ernest
Pittenger, Kenneth L.
Placencio, Martino
Plant, Guy E.
Porter, Jackson C.
Portis, Gordon K.
Portzline, Donald E.
Potts, Kenneth E.
Preis, Charles
Price, William M.
Prinder, Hubert R.
Provenson, James P.
Puches, Edmund M.

Radillo, Louis
Radziwon, Frank A.
Rahner, Harry B.
Rankin, Tom E.
Rannells, James M.
Ransom, William L.
Rasmus, Anthony R.
Reams, Robert J.
Rechel, Charles L.
Redic, Jack C.
Reed, Thomas J.
Reid, Richard H.
Reider, Raymond E.
Renaud, Albert A.
Repec, Flory
Repich, Joseph J., BS
Rhodes, Jesse C.
Richards, Forrest J.

Richardson, Gus W.
Richardson, Jack
Rieman, Gilbert F.
Rieth, Albert R., Jr.
Rife, Robert M.
Rittelmeyer, Ben V., KIA
Roane, William S., BS
Robert, Wilding E.
Roberts, James P.
Robertson, James
Rolland, Jee
Romanowski, Adolph P.
Roperti, Anthony
Rose, Billy M.
Ross, Samuel J.
Rovito, Albert J.
Ruetz, James W.

Sanchez, Joseph J.
Sander, Harlan R.
Sauls, Wilson M.
Savage, Willis G.
Sawyer, Melvin
Schieler, William F.
Schmidt, Joseph F.
Sciulli, Angelo
Scott, Roy D.
Sears, John
Sehnke, Donald H.
Sheehan, James E.
Sheehan, William F.
Sheely, Everett N.
Sheffield, Carl R.
Shemansky, Bernard J.
Shimko, Michael
Siehal, Gerald G.

Sieglitz, George W.
Simmons, Basil W., BS
Sinclair, George F.
Sinclair, Harold E.
Siratt, Ellis V.
Smith, Alfred N.
Smith, Donald L.
Smith, Francis
Smith, James T.
Smith, Joe F.
Snodgrass, Leonard E.
Snyder, Earl G.
Solak, Michael
Solla, Joseph A.
Spaulding, Malcolm W.
Spendio, Dominic L.
Stadelman, Joseph W.
Stahl, Robert S.
Stammer, Elmer L.
Staples, Robert W., Jr.
Starkey, Albert J.
Starkovich, Martin Jr.
Stearns, Landern R.
Steelman, Melvin S.
Stephens, Albert C.
Stephens, George J.
Stifflemire, Sherwood
Stoddard, Frederick
Storms, William H.
Stout, Daniel E.
Stroup, Russell A.
Sturgis, Richard F.
Sullivan, Edward J.
Swarthout, Warren H.
Syage, George J.
Syapin, John

Tarpley, Edward J.
Taylor, Jack G.
Taylor, William F.
Tesch, Raymond W.
Tesoriero, Patsy
Tessier, Arthur J.
Teutul, Emil H.
Tewell, Charles W.
Thomas, Noah B.
Thompson, John R.
Thompson, Robert J.
Thomson, Randolph M.
Tisdale, Robert L.
Todd, Loyd E.
Tom, Nichael J.
Tompkins, Hubert L., Jr.
Tonfne, Francis J.
Tranum, Richard A.
Travis, Harold W.
Trobaugh, Joseph H.
Truelove, Robert E.
Turcotte, Ray J.
Turmenne, Bernard A.
Turner, John A.
Tyner, Herman A.

Ucasz, Walter J.
Uenking, James K.
Uselman, John J.

Vanlandingham, G. P., DOW
Vant Hof, Robert C.,
Vasquez, Tony R.
Veinot, B. L.

Vetovich, John J.
Vincent, John D.
Viola, Gino L.
Voss, Jean H.
Vougioukas, A. T.

Wagoner, Marshals
Waldron, John C.
Waldron, Phillip F.
Walsh, John T.
Ward, John W.
Watkins, Thomas W.
Watson, Thomas J., Jr.
Weakley, Thomas A., Jr.
Weaver, Fred D.
Webler, George L.
Welch, Ross W.
Weldon, Lloyd E.
Wellman, Harold G.
Whalen, Thomas H.
Wheeler, Harry B.
Wieczorek, Remon
Wiedmann, Carl D.
Wiggens, James R.
Wiggins, Glenn R.
Wight, Charles N.
Wilde, Cyril H.
Wilhite, Tedd P.
Wilkerson, T. W. Jr,
Williams, Henry C.
Williams, Hinton O.
Williams, Ralph
Willman, Robert C.
Wilson, Armond G.
Wilson, Donald L.
Wilson, Kelley W.

Wilson, Robert L.
Winistorfer, George I.
Winnie, John W.
Winslow, James D.
Wiscarson, Eugene B.
Womble, Wallace H.
Woodard, Allen E.
Wooley, William L.
Wray, Leo B.
Wright, Bernard L.
Wright, Edward C.

Young, Johnnie C.
Young, Louis L.
Yount, Arthur W.

Zeman, Wesley J.
Zlotnick, George
Zouadjancik, Albert F.
Zylinski, Chester J.

Bibliography

Ailsby, Christopher. Hitler's Sky Warriors: German Paratroopers in Action (Staplehurst, UK: Spellmount Ltd, 2001).

Alexander, A. John and Arthur K. Marmon. "Combat Chronicle: An Outline History of U.S. Army Divisions," U.S. Department of the Army, Historical Division, Order of Battle Series, 1948.

Allen, Peter. One More River: The Rhine Crossings of 1945 (New York: Charles Scribner's Sons, 1980).

Ambrose, Stephen E. Band of Brothers: E Company, 506th Regiment, 101st Airborne from Normandy to Hitler's Eagle's Nest (New York: Simon & Schuster, 2001 Classic Edition).

Anderson, J.B. to W.M. Miley, April 24, 1945. "Miley, Official Correspondence, Received. January 24-July 26, 1945," William M. Miley Papers, Box 2. USAMHI.

Andrews, John. Airborne Album 1943-1945 Normandy to Victory (Williamstown, NJ: Phillips Publications, c.1992).

Anzuoni, Robert P. The All American: An Illustrated History of the 82nd Airborne Division, 1917 to the Present (Atglen, PA: Schiffer Military History, 2001).

Autry, Jerry, assisted by Kathryn Autry. General William C. Lee: Father of the Airborne: Just Plain Bill (San Francisco:, CA: Airborne Press, c. 1995).

Ayling, Keith. They Fly to Fight: The Story of Airborne Divisions (New York: D. Appleton, 1944).

Bando, Mark A. Vanguard of the Crusade: The 101st Airborne Division in World War II (Bedford, PA: Aberjona, 2003).

Barker, Geoffrey T. "Chronology U.S. Airborne Forces," in Bart Hagerman (ed) U.S.A. Airborne 50th Anniversary, 1940-1990 (Paducah, KY: Turner Publishing Co., 1990), 401-473.

Berkel, Alexander. Krieg vor der Eigenen Haustür: Rheinübergang und Luftlandung am Niederrhein 1945. Studien und Quellen zur Geschichte von Wesel 17 (Wesel: Stadtarchivs Wesel, 1994).

Biggs, Bradley. The Triple Nickels: America's First All-Black Paratroop Unit (Hamden, CT: Archon Books, 1986).

Bilstein, Roger E. Airlift and Airborne Operations in World War II (Air Force History and Museums Program, U.S. Government Printing Office, 1988).

Blair, Clay. Ridgway's Paratroopers: The American Airborne in World War II (New York: Dial Press, 1985).

Bowen, Robert. Fighting with the Screaming Eagles: With the 101st Airborne Division from Normandy to Bastogne (Mechanicsburg, PA: Stackpole Greenhill Military Books, 2004).

Bradley, Lt. Col. Francis X. and Lt. Col. H. Glen Wood. Paratrooper (Harrisburg, PA: The Military Service Publishing Company, 1954).

[Branigan, Jr., Edward S.] "History of Services, 464th Parachute Field Artillery Battalion," no date, "Rhine River Crossing. 17th ABN Div." Folder, William B. Breuer Papers, Box 3, World War II Units, 17th Airborne Division, USAMHI.

_____. "Operation Varsity Airborne Phase" May 3, 1945, "Rhine River Crossing. 17th ABN Div." Folder, William B. Breuer Papers, Box 3, World War II Units, 17th Airborne Division, USAMHI.

_____. "Awarded the Legion of Merit for Initiative," article clipping from unnamed periodical, February 1946, p. 15, "Rhine River Crossing. 17th ABN Div.," Folder, William B. Breuer Papers, Box 3, World War II Units 17th Airborne Division, USAMHI.

_____. To William B. Breuer, January 11, 1984.

212

Brereton, L.H. to M.B. Ridgway, April 3, 1945, "Miley, Official Correspondence between Gen. Brereton and Gen. Ridgway," William M. Miley Papers, Box 2. USAMHI.

Bressler, Dean M. "Allied Forces Breach the Rhine," Assembly 53 (1995): 21-27.

Breuer, William B. Collection, USAMHI.

_____. Storming Hitler's Rhine – The Allied Assault February—March 1945 (New York: St. Martins, 1985).

_____. Geronimo: American Paratroopers in World War II (New York: St. Martins, 1989).

Brown, Ashley and Jonathan Reed (eds) The Airborne (Harrisburg, PA: National Historical Society, c. 1989).

Burgett, Donald R. Currahee: A Paratrooper's Account of the Normandy Invasion (New York: Bantam, 1999).

_____. Beyond the Rhine: A Screaming Eagle in Germany (New York: Presidio, 2001).

_____. Road to Arnhem: A Screaming Eagle in Holland (New York: Dell, 2001).

"Camp Mackall: Home of the 'Airborne' in World War II." XVIII Airborne Corps & Fort Bragg. 6 April 2004 <http://www.bragg.army.mil/18abn/CampMackall.htm>.

Carter, Ross S. Those Devils in Baggy Pants (Canton, OH: Claymore Publishing, 1979 reprint of 1951 edition).

Cioc, Mark. The Rhine: An Eco-Biography, 1815-2000 (Seattle: University of Washington Press, 2002).

Clancy, Tom. Airborne: A Guided Tour of an Airborne Task Force (New York: Diane Publishing Co., 1997).

Clark, Alan. The Fall of Crete (London: Cassell, 2002).

Cooper, Alan. Wot? No Engines!: RAF Glider Pilots and Operation Varsity (Bognor Regis, U.K.: Woodfield Publishing, 2002).

Crookenden, Napier. Airborne at War (Shepperton, Surrey: Ian Allan, 1978).

D'Ambra, Al. "The Cigarette Camps: The U.S. Army Camps in the Le Havre Area." September 2002. 225th AAA Searchlight Battalion Veterans Association. 24 May 2004 <http://www.skylighters.org/special/cigcamps/cmplstrk.html>.

[Davis], Pat. <u>American Light Infantry Battles: Paratroopers, 1942-1945</u> (Reseda, CA, c. 1997).

Densman, Pat, "Jumping Gyrenes," <u>The Leatherneck</u> (Nov. 1941): 8-9, 12-13, 84-86.

Devlin, Gerard M. <u>Paratrooper: The Saga of U.S. Army and Marine Parachute and Glider Combat Troops During World War II</u> (New York: St. Martins, 1979).

_____. <u>Silent Wings. The Saga of the U.S. Army and Marine Combat Glider Pilots During World War II</u> (New York: St. Martins Press, 1985).

"Document on Joint Airborne Operations," (Ft. Bragg, N.C.: Joint Airborne Troop Board, June 18, 1954).

Duncan, Gregory. <u>Dick Donnelly of the Paratroops</u> (Racine, WI: Whitman Publishing Co., 1944).

Edwards, Roger. <u>German Airborne Troops, 1936-45</u> (Garden City, NY: Double Day, 1974).

Eisenhower, Dwight D., Supreme Commander, Allied Expeditionary Force. "Report on Operations in Northwest Europe, 6 June 1944 – 8 May 1945," USAMHI.

_____. <u>Crusade in Europe</u> (Garden City, New York: Doubleday, 1948).

Eldridge, Major Justin L.C. "Defense on the Rhine," <u>Military Intelligence</u> 21 (1995): 38- 44, 52.

<u>Employment of Airborne and Troop Carrier Forces</u> (Fort Leavenworth, Kansas: Command and General Staff School, 1944).

<u>Establishment and Operation of a Parachute School in a Theater of Operations</u>, Prepared under the Direction of the Commandant (Ft. Benning, Georgia: The Parachute School, March 1943).

Farrar-Hockley, Anthony H. <u>Airborne Carpet: Operation Market Garden</u> (NY: Ballantine Books, 1969).

Ferguson, Arthur W. <u>Jump Happy</u> (New York: Privately Printed, 1942).

Fiebig, Major General Heinz. "The 84th Infantry Division During the Fights from Reichswald to Wesel," Foreign MS B-843, USAMHI.

"Field Order No. 5 for Operation Varsity," Headquarters IX Troop Carrier Command U.S. Army Air Forces, March 16, 1945.

Fitzgerald, Lt. Charles B. "Paratrooper Training," The Marine Corps Gazette 27 (1943): 13-18.

Flanagan, E.M. Jr. Airborne: A Combat History of American Airborne Forces (New York: Presidio, 2002).

Flory, Robert A. "Churchill's Secret," Airborne Quarterly 9 (1996): 7.

Forster, Greg. "Biggest Wartime Airdrop," Military History 11 (1994): 38-44.

"464th Battalion leaves IRTC after serving here four months," Unidentified newspaper clipping, authors' collection.

Fowle, Barry W. "The Rhine River Crossings," in Barry W. Fowle (ed) Builders and Fighters: U.S. Army Engineers in World War II (Fort Belvoir, Virginia: Office of History, United States Army Corps of Engineers, 1992), pp. 463-475.

François, Dominique. The 508th Parachute Infantry Regiment: Red Devils: Normandy-Ardennes-Germany (Bayeux, France: Editions Heimdal, 2003).

_____. 82nd Airborne in Normandy: A History in Period Photographs (Atglen, PA: Schiffer Military History, 2004).

Friedheim, Eric. "Rhineland Rendezvous," Air Force 28 (1945): 4-6, 28, 58.

Gable, Kurt. The Making of a Paratrooper: Airborne Training and Combat in World War II (Lawrence: University of Kansas Press, 1990).

Garrett, Scott. "Airborne Through the Ages," in Bart Hagerman (ed) U.S.A. Airborne 50th Anniversary, 1940-1990 (Paducah, KY: Turner Publishing Co, 1990), pp. 25 – 69.

Gavin, James M. Airborne Warfare (Washington, DC: Infantry Journal Press, 1947).

_____. On to Berlin: Battles of an Airborne Commander 1943-1946 (New York: Viking, 1978).

General of the Army. "Supreme Commanders Dispatch for Operations in Northwest Europe, 6 June 1944 – 8 May 1945."

Gilbert, Martin. The Day the War Ended: May 8, 1945 – Victory in Europe (New York: Holt, 1995).

Gregory, Barry. United States Airborne Forces (New York: Gallery Books, 1990).

_____. and John Batchelor. <u>Airborne Warfare 1918-1945</u> (New York, Exeter Books, 1979).

Hagerman, Bart (ed). <u>U.S.A. Airborne 50th Anniversary,1940-1990</u> (Paducah, KY: Turner Publishing Co, 1990).

_____. "Operation Varsity: The Airborne Assault over the Rhine," in Bart Hagerman (ed) <u>U.S.A. Airborne 50th Anniversary, 1940-1990</u> (Paducah, KY: Turner Publishing Co., 1990), 129-137.

_____. "17th Airborne Division," in B. Hagerman (ed) <u>U.S.A. Airborne 50th Anniversary, 1940-1990</u> (Paducah, KY: Turner Publishing Co., 1990), 151-152.

_____. (ed) <u>War Stories: The Men of the Airborne</u> (Paducah, KY: Turner Publishing Co., 1993).

_____. "General Miley and 'His' Division," <u>The Airborne Quarterly</u> 10 (1997): 18-25.

_____. "Operation Varsity Airborne Bridge Across the Rhine," <u>World War II</u> 12 (1998): 50-56.

_____. "The 17th Airborne Division . . . 'WWII's Forgotten Troopers'," <u>The Airborne Quarterly</u> 15(2002): 151-152.

Hall, Tony (ed). <u>March to Victory: The Final Months of WWII from D-Day, June 6, 1944 to the Fall of Japan, August 14, 1945</u> (New York: Crescent Books, 1994).

Harclerode, Peter. <u>Wings of War: Airborne Warfare 1918-1945</u> (London: Weidenfeld and Nicolson, 2005).

Heydte, Baron von der. <u>Daedalus Returned</u> (Littleton, CO: Aberdeen Books, 2001 reprint).

Hickey, Michael. <u>Out of the Sky: A History of Airborne Warfare</u>, (New York: Charles Scribner's Sons, 1979).

Hinson, Wade C. to Robert L. Wilson, December 13, 2003.

"Historical Report of Operation Varsity," 17th Airborne Division, 1945.

Hottelet, Richard C. "Big Jump into Germany," <u>Collier's</u>, May 5, 1945, as reprinted in <u>Reporting World War II. Part II: American Journalism, 1944-1946</u> (New York: The Library of America, 1995).

Hoyt, Edwin P. <u>Airborne: A History of American Parachute Forces</u> (New York: Stein and Day, 1979).

Jacobus, George R. (ed) <u>Echoes of the Warriors: Personal Experiences of the Enlisted Men and Officers of E Company of the 505th Parachute Infantry Regiment, 82nd Airborne in World War II</u> (George R. Jacobus, 1992).

Jones, Robert. <u>101st Airborne Division</u> (Paducah, KY: Turner Publishing Co., 1997).

Kennett, Lee. <u>GI: The American Soldier in World War II</u> (New York: Charles Scribner's Sons, 1987).

Killblane, Richard and Jake McNeice. <u>The Filthy Thirteen: From the Dustbowl to Hitler's Eagles Nest: The 101st Airborne's Most Legendary Squad of Combat Paratroopers</u> (Havertown, PA: Casemate, 2003).

Kormann, John G. "Another View of Operation Varsity," <u>The Airborne Quarterly</u> 14 (2001): 12-13.

Kurtz, Robert. <u>German Paratroops: Uniforms, Insignia, and Equipment of the Fallschirmjäger in World War II</u> (Atglen, PA: Schiffer, 2000).

Langston, Frank and Justin P. Buckridge (eds). <u>The Talon Crosses the Rhine</u> (Paris: E. Desfossés-Néogravure, 1945).

Larson, George. "13th Airborne Division: 'Thrice Called, Thrice Denied,'" <u>The Airborne Quarterly</u> 15 (2002): 46-50.

Lassen, Don and Richard K. Schrader. <u>Pride of America: An Illustrated History of the U.S. Airborne Forces</u> (Missoula, Montana: Pictorial Histories Publishing Co., 1991).

Lowden, John L. <u>Silent Wings at War: Combat Gliders in World War II</u> (Washington, D.C.: Smithsonian Institution Press, 1992).

Lucas, James. <u>Storming Eagles: German Airborne Forces in World War II</u> (London: Cassell, 2001).

MacDonald, Charles. <u>Airborne</u> (New York: Ballantine, 1970).

Maclean, Norman. <u>Young Men and Fire</u> (Chicago: The University of Chicago Press, 1992).

Magill, John F. <u>We Led From The Sky: A Combat Paratrooper's Story</u> ('Computer Printed,' c. 1998), WWII Veteran's Survey, "17th Airborne Division," Box, "Magill, John. F" Folder. USAMHI.

Marr, John. "507th Parachute Infantry Regiment," in Bart Hagerman (ed) <u>U.S.A. Airborne 50th Anniversary, 1940-1990</u> (Paducah, KY: Turner Publishing Co., 1990), pp. 264-277.

McKee, Alexander. The Race for the Rhine Bridges: 1940-1944-1945 (NY: Stein and Day, 1971).

McNab, Chris. German Paratroopers: The History of the Fallschirmjäger in WWII (St. Paul, MN: MBI Publishing Co., 2000).

Megellas, James. All the Way to Berlin: A Paratrooper in World War II Europe (New York: Ballantine, 2003).

Miley, Major General William B. "Memorandum," March 27, 1945., in George L. Streuker's Papers, Box 1, "After Action Report Maps, 17th Airborne Division, 1945" Folder. USAMHI.

_____. "Varsity, Background Information," March 10, 1945., Annex 1a to Field Order No. 1., sheet 2 of 3. USAMHI.

_____. "Directive to Germans in the area under control of the 17th Division, April 19, 1945, Miley, Official Correspondence, Sent. April 19-August 1, 1945," William M. Miley Papers, Box 2. USAMHI.

Mitchell, David T. and Sharon L. Snyder (eds). The Body and Physical Difference: Discourses of Disability (Ann Arbor, MI: University of Michigan Press, 1997).

Mitchell, William C. "Epilogue. One Last Great Jump: Operation Varsity," in Kurt Gable, The Making of a Paratrooper: Airborne Training and Combat in World War II (Lawrence: University of Kansas Press, 1990), pp. 254-272.

Moran, Jeff. American Airborne Pathfinders in World War II (Atglen, PA: Schiffer Publishing, Ltd, 2003).

Morgan, Martin K.A. Down To Earth: The 50th Parachute Infantry Regiment in Normandy, June 6-July 11, 1944 (Atglen, PA: Schiffer Military History, 2004).

Moses, Lloyd R. to W.M.Miley, April 22, 1945. "Miley, Official Correspondence, Received. January 24 - July 26, 1945," William M. Miley Papers, Box 2. USAMHI.

Murray, Williamson. "Airborne Comes of Age," World War II 18 (2004): 26- 42.

Myer, Samuel C. "Varsity's Organic Artillery," Field Artillery Journal, 35 (1945): 673 -676.

"Narrative of Operation Varsity 24 March 1945," 1945.

Nelson, Mark J. With the Black Devils: A Soldier's WWII Account with the First Special Service Force and the 82nd Airborne (Atglen, PA: Schiffer Military History, 2003).

Nitrowski, Johann J. Die Luftlandung und das Kriegsende im Gebiet der Städte Hamminkeln und Wesel (Hamminkeln: Stadt Hamminkeln, 1997).

Nolan, Keith William. Ripcord: Screaming Eagles Under Siege, Vietnam 1970 (Novato, CA: Presidio Press, 2000).

O'Neil, William. A Democracy at War: America's Fight at Home and Abroad in World War II (New York: Free Press, 1993).

"Operation Varsity 23 March, 1945 to 30 March 1945," XVIII Corps (Airborne).

"Operational Diary, 17th Airborne Division Covering January 1, 1945 to April 10, 1945."

Organized Reserve Corps Airborne Training Course, Eighty Second Airborne Division, Fort Bragg, North Carolina (1941).

Pandak, Bill to William B. Breuer (n.d.), "Correspondence with Veterans of Division Artillery, 17th Airborne Division" Folder, William B.Breuer Papers, Box 3. USAMHI.

Paratroop Training (Ft. Benning, GA, 1944).

Pay, Donald R. "Operational Diary 17th Airborne Division Covering January 1, 1945 to April 10, 1945," Published under the auspices of the 19th Airborne Division Association, St. Paul, MN: Mel Therrien, 1993.

_____. Thunder From Heaven: Story of the 17th Airborne Division 1943-1945 (Nashville, TN: Battery Press, 1980 reprint).

Peatling, Robert. Without Tradition: 2 Para, 1941-1945 (Barnsley, U.K.: Pen and Sword, 2004).

Pimlott, John. "Crossing the Rhine," in Tony Hall (ed) March to Victory: The Final Months of WWII from D-Day, June 6, 1944 to the Fall of Japan, August 14, 1945 (New York: Crescent Books, 1994), pp.129-145.

Polk, David. World War II Army Airborne Troop Carriers (Paducah, KY: Turner Publishing Co, 1992).

"Prediction of Success and Failure of Paratroopers Based on Background and Training Data." U.S. War Department. Troop Information and Education Division, 18 October 1945.

"Prop Blast," Newsletter of the 517th Parachute Infantry, Camp Mackall, N.C.

Quarrie, Barrie. German Airborne Troops, 1939-45 (London: Osprey Publications, 1983).

_____. Airborne Assault: Parachute Forces in Action, 1940-1991 (Somerset, United Kingdom: Patrick Stevens, Ltd., 1991).

Raff, Colonel Edson D. We Jump To Fight (NY: Eagle, 1944).

Ramsey, Winston G. "Operation Plunder," in After the Battle, No. 16 (London: Battle of Britain Prints International, Ltd, 1977), pp. 15-27.

"Report of the Allied Air Operations in Preparation for and in Connection with Operations 'Plunder' and 'Varsity,'" Supreme Headquarters, Allied Expeditionary Force, Office of the Assistant Chief of Staff, March 28, 1945.

"Report of Operation Varsity to Supreme Commander, Allied Expeditionary Forces," Headquarters, First Allied Airborne Army, 1945.

Reporting World War II. Part II: American Journalism, 1944-1946 (New York: The Library of America, 1995).

Ridgway, Matthew B. to W.M. Miley, March 29, 1945, "Miley, Official Correspondence, Received. January 24-July 26, 1945," William M. Miley Papers, Box 2. USAMHI.

_____. "An Airborne Corps Operation," Military Review 25 (1945): 14-16.

_____. Soldier: The Memoirs of Matthew B. Ridgway (New York: Harper, 1956).

Ross, Kirk B. The Skymen: A Parachute Rifle Company's Story of the Battle of the Bulge and the Jump Across the Rhine (Atglen, PA: Schiffer Military History, 2000).

Ryan, Cornelius. A Bridge Too Far (New York: Simon & Schuster, 1974).

Sampson, Francis L. Look Out Below: A Story of the Airborne by a Paratrooper Padre (Washington, D.C.: Catholic University of America Press, 1948).

Saunders, Tim. Nijmegen: Market Garden – U.S. 82nd Airborne Division, 1944 (Barnsley, U.K.: Pen and Sword, 2001).

Sebag-Montefiore, Hugh. Enigma: The Battle for the Code (New York: John Wiley, 2001).

"17th Airborne Division Historical Report of Operation Varsity," 1945.

Sharma, H. Rex. Pulse and Repulse: Troop Carrier and Airborne Teams in Europe during World War II (Austin, TX: Eakin, 1995).

Smith, W. Thomas, Jr. Alpha Bravo Delta Guide to American Airborne Forces (New York: Alpha Books, 2004).

Steer, Frank. Arnhem: The Fight to Sustain: The Untold Story of the Airborne Logisticians (Barnsley, U.K.: Pen & Sword, 2001).

Stevenson, Frank E. "Third Army's Planning for the Crossing of the Rhine River," Military Review 30 (1951): 33-42.

Stock, James W. Rhine Crossing (New York: Ballantine Books, 1973).

"Summary of Ground Forces Participation in Operation 'Varsity,' 25 March 1945," XVIII Corps (Airborne) Operation Varsity 23 March, 1945 to 30 March 1945, 1945.

"Tactical and Non-Tactical Operations During the Final Phase of the War in Europe, including Operation 'Varsity'" Headquarters, IX Carrier Command, 1945.

Taylor, Thomas. Lightning in the Storm: The 101st Air Assault Division in the Gulf War (New York: Hippocrene, 2003).

"13th Airborne Division, Training History," c.1946, USAMHI.

Thompson, Jack. Charleston at War: The Photographic Record 1860-1865 (Gettysburg: Thomas Publications, 2000).

Thompson, Leroy. U.S. Airborne in Action. Combat Troops Number 10. (Carrollton, TX: Squadron/Signal Publications, Inc., 1992).

"Thousands Greet Sky Troopers and Buy Bonds," Unidentified newspaper clipping, authors' collection.

Timmes, Charles J. "Development of the Parachute and Airborne Activities in the U.S.S.R.," June 1952 typescript, USAMHI.

Toguchi, Robert M. "The Evolution of United States Army River Crossing Doctrine and Equipment, 1918-45," Ph.D. Dissertation, Duke University, 1994.

Tom, William. "17th Airborne Division@miltary.com. August 16 2000. Military.com Unit Pages. 5 February 2004 http://www.miltary.

com/HomePage/UnitPageHistory/1,13506,700490/702423,0
0.html>.

"USAF Airborne Operations. World War II and Korean War," USAF
Historical Division Liaison Office, March 1962.

"USS General William Weigel, AP-119." U.S. Coast Guard. August 2001
<http://www.uscg.mil/hq/g-cp/history/WEBCUTTERS/G_
Weigel.html>.

"U.S. Trains More Parachute Troops," Life (May 12, 1941), 110-117.

Verier, Mike. 82nd Airborne Division "All American," Spearhead volume
4 (Hersham, Surrey: Ian Allan, 2001).

War News: The Magazine of the Warfront and the Homefront, Special
Publication of the Mid Atlantic Air Museum's 13th Annual
WW II Weekend, June 2004.

Webster, David Kenyon. Parachute Infantry: An American Paratrooper's
Memoir of D -Day and the Fall of the Third Reich (New York:
Delta, 2002).

Weeks, John. Airborne Equipment: A History of Its Development
(New York: Hippocrene Books, 1976).

White, Ced. "A Paratrooper," 508th, No 3. 1942, "The 508th" Folder,
William M. Miley Papers, Box 1. 1942. USAMHI.

White, Captain John A. "Parachute Troops," The Marine Corps Gazette
24 (1940): 11 -14.

Whiting, Charles. Hunters From the Sky: The German Parachute
Corps 1940-1945 (New York: Stein and Day, 1974).

_____. Bounce the Rhine (Havertown, PA: Casemate, 2002).

Wilson, James C. "A WWII Paratrooper's Story," essay submitted to
the Hershey Museum's 2003-04 History Contest, Hershey,
Pennsylvania, 2004.

Wilson, Robert L. and Philip K. Wilson, "Operation Varsity: 17th
Airborne Crosses the Rhine March 24, 1945. One Participant's
Perspective," 2004.

Wolfe, Martin. Green Light! Men of the 81st Troop Carrier Squadron
Tell Their Story (Philadelphia: University of Pennsylvania
Press, 1989).

Zinsmeister, Karl. Boots on the Ground: A Month with the 82nd
Airborne in the Battle for Iraq (New York: Truman Talley
Books, 2003).

Index

Montgolfier, Etienne 2
Montgomery, Bernard L. 99, 103, 113, 114, 115, 119, 122, 137, 141, 142, 143, 152, 185
Moses, Lloyd R. 183, 218
Murrow, Edward R. 112

Neufchateau, France 172, 173
Normandy ix, x, 6, 81, 84, 107, 114, 146, 166, 181, 211, 212, 213, 215, 218

Operation Merker 7
Operation Plunder 113, 119, 120, 122, 151, 220
Operation Rype 122
Operation Torch 71
Operation Varsity iii, xiii, xiv, 7, 94, 96, 98, 99, 100, 108, 111, 112, 113, 116, 117, 118, 119, 120, 122, 123, 124, 128, 131, 132, 134, 135, 136, 137, 138, 139, 141, 143, 146, 148, 149, 150, 151, 152, 155, 162, 170, 172, 179, 180, 181, 182, 185, 213, 214, 216, 217, 218, 219, 220, 221, 222
Oscar 56, 81, 194, 198

Pandak, William 103, 104, 107, 204, 219
Pathfinder 123
Patton, George S. 122, 185
Pay, Donald R. 94, 155, 156, 158, 186, 192, 219
Pearl Harbor 24, 25
Phelps, J. W. 96
Pimlott, John 100, 114, 219

Raff, Edson D. 1, 96, 97, 144, 145, 150, 186, 220
Rhine River iii, vii, x, xiii, 7, 83, 94, 98, 99, 100, 101, 103, 111, 113, 114, 119, 120, 121, 122, 124, 126, 128, 129, 130, 131, 133, 134, 135, 138, 139, 141, 142, 144, 145, 148, 150, 152, 155, 158, 164, 168, 172, 180, 181, 182, 183, 184, 185, 187, 188, 190, 211, 212, 213, 214, 215, 216, 217, 218, 219, 220, 221, 222
Ridgway, Matthew B. ix, xii, 58, 88, 93, 97, 111, 113, 117, 119, 123, 142, 144, 162, 180, 181, 182, 183, 212, 213, 220
Ritchie, Neil 113
Rozier, Pilâtre de 2
Ryder, William T. 7